I0481151

Cryptocurrency Investing Bible

The Ultimate Guide to Unlock the Secrets of Bitcoin, Blockchain and Cryptocurrency, Bitcoin Investment Tips for Success

Leon Watson

This bundle contains following books:

1. Bitcoin Investment Basics - Tips for Success (Mastering Bitcoin for Starters)

2. Blockchain: The Ultimate Guide to Understanding the Technology Behind Bitcoin and Cryptocurrency (Including Blockchain Wallet, Mining, Bitcoin, Ethereum, Litecoin, Ripple, Dash and Smart Contracts)

Book 1

Bitcoin Investment Basics - Tips for Success

Mastering Bitcoin for Starters

Leon Watson

including specific information will be considered an illegal act irrespective of if it is done electronically or in print. This extends to creating a secondary or tertiary copy of the work or a recorded copy and is only allowed with express written consent from the Publisher. All additional rights reserved.

The information in the following pages is broadly considered to be a truthful and accurate account of facts and as such any inattention, use or misuse of the information in question by the reader will render any resulting actions solely under their purview. There are no scenarios in which the publisher or the original author of this work can be in any fashion deemed liable for any hardship or damages that may befall them after undertaking information described herein.

Additionally, the information in the following pages is intended only for informational purposes and should thus be thought of as universal. As befitting its nature, it is presented without assurance regarding its prolonged validity or interim quality. Trademarks that are mentioned are done without written consent and can in no way be considered an endorsement from the trademark holder.

x

TABLE OF CONTENTS

Introduction

Congratulations on downloading *"Bitcoin Investment Basics - Tips for Success (Mastering Bitcoin for Starters)"* and thank you for doing so. Bitcoin and blockchain, the underlying technology that makes it possible, are literally game changing technologies that are already having a major effect on everything from the financial industry to the way that supply chain infrastructure works. While that is all well and good, if you are like most investors then what matters most to you is that it is also making plenty of speculators extraordinarily rich in the interim.

While there is certainly money to be made in Bitcoin, there is more to the process than simply trading your cash for Bitcoins and wishing really hard, which is why the following chapters will discuss everything you need to know in order to strike while the cryptocurrency iron is hot. First, you will learn all about what Bitcoin is exactly, its history, and why you should care about it. Next, you will learn all about the ways in which Bitcoin, and other cryptocurrencies, attain their price on the open market. You will then learn about the main competitors to Bitcoin's dominance of the cryptocurrency market.

From there you will learn all about how to get started with Bitcoin, including finding a bitcoin wallet and choosing an exchange. You will then learn all about investing in bitcoins, both by investing in them directly in a traditional fashion and also by investing in a cloud mining service. With that out of the way you will then learn about many of the types of fraud that you will be facing when dealing with cryptocurrency, as well as tips to ensure you don't become a victim. Finally, you will learn some tips for success to ensure that your time investing in bitcoins is as profitable as possible.

There are plenty of books on this subject on the market, thanks again for choosing this one! Every effort was made to ensure it is full of as much useful information as possible, please enjoy!

Chapter 1: Bitcoin Basics

These days, you don't need to be deeply tuned into the comings and goings of the investment markets, or the tech sector, to feel as though you are constantly hearing about Bitcoin everywhere you go. If everything you have heard up to this point has only served to make you more confused, rather than less, the good news is you aren't alone. Despite their seeming pervasiveness, only about 50 percent of the population can accurately describe what a bitcoin is, and only about 12 percent regularly interact with it on any sort of consistent basis. The short answer is that Bitcoin can be thought of as a digital platform to trade bitcoins (with a lowercase b) to other people in exchange for anything that a traditional currency could be traded for. Broadly speaking, it is similar to PayPal except it is using its own currency rather than the currency of a given country.

Bitcoin is what is known as a cryptocurrency, which means that unlike traditional, fiat, currencies, its price is purely based on what the market says that it is worth. Each transaction is then verified by a third party, known as a bitcoin miner, before then being added to the Bitcoin blockchain, a sort of digital ledger and database all in one, that makes Bitcoin possible. To understand blockchain technology, it is helpful to understand exactly how bitcoins function.

In addition to storing unique and group data, each block in a blockchain also contains a timestamp as well as other organizational information that lets the chain determine its overall place in the whole. Each blockchain network is also notable due to the fact that it contains no centralized server or authority in charge of making sure things work the way they should. Instead, these processes are spread among everyone using a blockchain which means a single blockchain could easily be spread across thousands of independent data nodes.

When a new transaction occurs, it is checked for authenticity and accuracy by a private individual known as a bitcoin miner. This individual then makes use of the bitcoin blockchain and verifies the new information that is stored in a specific block to ensure it aligns with all of the previous blocks. For their effort, the miner then receives a fraction of a total bitcoin to compensate them for their work. This process of unbiased, third-party verification is a key component of what makes a decentralized database possible.

Despite the fact that the database information is spread around the world with no central authority, and the fact that sections of it are inspected by third parties on a regular basis, the data that is stored in a blockchain remains incredibly secure. This level of security doesn't come from an active offense against fraud, it comes from the defensive capabilities of the way in which the blockchain is constructed.

As such, if someone wanted to utilize fraud on a blockchain network, say by using the same bitcoins to make two different transactions, they would need to generate enough false transactions that showed that the coins were not used the first time to ensure that 51 percent of the total transactions showed the false details as opposed to the true ones. This type of endeavor would be extremely cost prohibitive and require obscene amounts of energy, essentially making it more trouble than it is worth.

Inauspicious start

First appearing in 2008, the original vision for the original cryptocurrency was a way for people to send payments to one another without getting any financial institutions involved. This idea came from a paper written by a person or group of persons using the alias Satoshi Nakamoto and was titled *bitcoin: A Peer-to Peer Electronic Cash System.* This was followed in early 2009 by the original proof of concept and code which was also distributed via the Nakamoto pseudonym. The code was released in an open source format with numerous developers working on improving the code after all trace of Nakamoto vanished in 2010. However, rumors persist of a link hidden online somewhere that accesses Nakamoto's store of bitcoins worth an estimated one billion dollars.

In 2014, when bitcoin was first making a big splash amongst mainstream investors, programmers learned how to add a unique type of code to individual blocks to allow them to carry out specific tasks. This type of code is known as "smart contracts" and they are discussed in detail in a later chapter. Smart contracts are useful in a wide variety of scenarios, from facilitating contract negotiation to tracking patients in a hospital and their inclusion in the blockchain bag of tricks has cemented it as a technology to watch moving forward.

Most recently Bitcoin has been dealing with fallout relating to a 2013 Homeland Security ruling that placed bitcoin exchanges in the same categories as other money-changing agencies. This led to additional government oversight and a 2017 ruling by the Securities and Exchange Commission that denied Bitcoin the right to create an officially licensed bitcoin exchange that would operate under the purview of the federal government. As of the end of 2017 this ruling is still being appealed.

This ruling has left Bitcoin in a somewhat odd position as its increasing popularity has generated a demand for additional government oversight, yet this type of oversight is directly in opposition to the core tenants that were crucial to its creation. Additionally, while the rate at which new users are accessing Bitcoin is increasing, the number of individuals using the service is not yet great enough to organize an effective effort to ensure things stay the same. What's more, if these issues aren't solved before a point of mass saturation is reached, it is unlikely that they will ever be solved in the most efficient way possible.

In order for bitcoins to reach the level of mainstream adoption that they are capable of reaching, and truly become part of the existing financial system rather than operating alongside it, authorities in the space will need to uncover a way for the system to maintain its original purpose while at the same time evolving in such a way that it is accessible to a wide group of people. At the same time, it will need to ensure that its security doesn't change and that it retains enough of its decentralized nature to be recognizable when compared to its current form. Along the way it will also need to come up with a reasonable way to limit illicit activities without stifling other aspects of the anonymous nature in the process. As such, the future of Bitcoin is likely some amalgamation of the current form and something more akin to fiat currency.

Bitcoin transactions: Each bitcoin user can send a transaction to any other bitcoin user once they have saved that user's public bitcoin address. This address is then stored in the form of a cryptographic key to ensure that no one without the corresponding access code can see the full details of the transaction. To start a transaction, the sender's account sends a message to the receiver's account based on the key that was provided. The private key of the sender is then used to verify where the transaction came from. This signature will then also be used at a later point to determine just where the transaction started from. The transaction is then sent to a local node where it is collected with other transactions into a block that is then subjected to the mining process that is discussed in a later chapter.

Advantages of bitcoin: Compared to other, more traditional, types of transaction systems, bitcoin has several natural advantages. The first of these is that it eliminates the middleman entirely. By cutting out the cost and the delay associated with these types of transactions, bitcoin transactions can be completed in minutes rather than days. What's more, each transaction that takes place on the blockchain is naturally going to be visible to anyone who was a part of it, while also ensuring that relevant private information is properly concealed. This provides an extreme level of transparency that is hard to find in any other database or digital ledger.

The Bitcoin platform is also extremely popular due to its strong dedication to personal freedoms. Each transaction also has the option to be marked as private which means even fewer details are shared, even amongst those who otherwise have access to transaction details. Again, when compared to more traditional financial services, bitcoin places control of their privacy in the hands of the users which allows them to determine which details they are comfortable sharing and with whom.

Finally, bitcoin is already being called an outstanding means of stimulating financial innovation by those in the know. This is due to the fact that the Bitcoin protocol, and the blockchain technology that makes it possible are both open source which means that anyone can take the underlying code and do anything they want with it, free of charge.

Additionally, due to the fact that bitcoins are really just a record of ownership based on specific values, they can be very easily altered to serve as an indication of ownership interests outside of their more traditional uses.

As an example, they can be used as a means of measuring ownership when it comes to things like shares of businesses, intellectual property or ownership shares akin to those associated with a company's stock. Additionally, the bitcoin blockchain can undertake new protocols on top of the existing protocols to extend this functionality even further. Additional protocols typically include things like enhanced notary functionality or increase encryption options.

Chapter 2: Cryptocurrency Pricing Explained

While the unit price of bitcoin isn't controlled by any single entity, that doesn't mean it still isn't subject to the rules of supply and demand. As such, the unit price of bitcoin is always going to reflect the value that the market has assigned to it. From there, the only thing that will directly affect the price further is what speculators think about the current situation. In fact, it is one of the most straightforward examples of free market principles in play today. This is not to say that external events aren't going to affect the price. In fact, they are more likely to be affected by a wider variety of issues, as anything that speculators get up in arms about has the potential to cause a measurable change in price.

External factors also play a bigger role in the unit price of bitcoins than they do in traditional currencies, simply due to the fact that there are fewer filters between these forces and the market that drives them. Those who spend their days trading cryptocurrencies also often play a measurable role in the determination of price, especially among the smaller types of cryptocurrency. Cryptocurrency traders work just like any other type of trader in that they purchase a given currency and hold onto it for a varying length of time in hopes that the price will rise and they will profit from their investment. If enough individuals purchase and hold onto a specific currency, then they can conspire to drive the price to levels that are higher than demand and general usefulness otherwise would.

This scenario is what is known as a pricing bubble and bitcoin and other cryptocurrencies have already proven extremely vulnerable to its influences. While pricing bubbles are generally written off as a bad thing across the board, the truth of the matter is that they are only bad for those who bought into the current bubble once it had inflated well past the point where any profit could realistically be expected. People in this situation are usually those who heard about the current pricing boom and were eager to jump in without doing the proper amount of research beforehand. As long as you are aware of the possibility of a pricing bubble, and act accordingly, there is nothing preventing you from coming out ahead.

It is also possible for negative market forces to work together to push the price of bitcoin lower than what the market value is currently determining its worth to be. While this hasn't happened in some time, if it does occur then there are several counter forces that can be mustered to force the price back to a more accurate point.

News coverage: One of the easiest ways to ensure that the unit price of bitcoin is going to increase is to increase the amount of news coverage Bitcoin is currently receiving. Increased news coverage is a great way to manipulate the public into a buying frenzy by giving them something new to focus on. An increase in attention of this type almost always leads to an increase in price as new users finally decide that now is the time to take the plunge, decreasing supply and increasing the price as a result.

The media is known to take additional interest in topics such as bitcoin being added to a new exchange, an update to the existing code or anything that can put a face on this new financial trend. Additionally, it is a safe bet that the media will always make use of a great soundbite, especially something that shows the cryptocurrency market as a whole is expanding. The more coverage that is received in a shorter period of time, the more the price is going to rise. It really is that simple.

Grass roots concerns: While an increase in media coverage is great for a quick burst of unit price, the most effective long-term means of improving price lies in cultivating a dedicated following at the grass roots level. The bitcoin faithful are the ones that have been using the cryptocurrency for years and, while they may not have yet made their fortune, they are still going to be the ones who go out of their way to spread the good word in as many different venues as possible. The goodwill of this type of supporter is extremely valuable as they often take part in moves that generate artificial inflation in bitcoin's price. They are also the ones the most likely to help out with coding, provide valuable feedback and, of course, put their own money into bitcoin as well.

A great example of this can be seen in the bitcoin pricing bubble of 2014, the most severe pricing bubble that bitcoin had seen prior to the 2017 pricing bubble. The 2014 pricing bubble occurred at a time when traditional investors were first starting to take notice. This was also the first time that Bitcoin reached a level of mass adoption that was strong enough for word of mouth to really take off. Then, within a few months, investors of all sorts were soon talking about something that had previously just been used to buy drugs online and suddenly the price of bitcoin was greater than $1,000 per unit.

Social media: While traditional types of investments typically break important announcements via social media, when it comes to cryptocurrency *all* the big news happens in the social media space. Despite being a decentralized database, Bitcoin has a strong social media presence with thousands of groups dedicated to supporting the cryptocurrency, and making money from its every movement which means that all it would take is the idea that some big piece of news is about to break in order to get movement started one way or another. What's more interesting is that trends of this sort will tend to start at just the suggestion of the rumor, regardless of whether or not anything actually comes of it which means many of these rumors simply end up being self-fulfilling prophecies.

Liquidity: Another common way that price is influenced is through means that artificially increase liquidity. A majority of this artificial liquidity is created by Chinese bots who simply do nothing but move bitcoins back and forth with one another. This, in turn, helps to ensure that public interest of some type is always on Bitcoin and ensures that the price retains a steady rate. Liquidity also refers to the amount of an asset that is available to trade. If liquidity is low then those who are looking to buy bitcoins will be unable to do so.

In order to ensure that there is always enough supply to meet the required demand, the transactions that the bots create are then mined, adding new bitcoins to the blockchain in the process. Every time enough transactions are generated to fill a block; 12.5 new bitcoins are generated, and this takes place hundreds of times every day.

These types of tactics are often used by those who have one type of vested interest or another in keeping the price of bitcoin as high as possible. This is often done by those who are looking to initiate what is known as a "pump and dump". To initiate a pump and dump an investor needs to buy up the entire available supply of bitcoins, which is easier than it sounds. This is because they don't need to buy up all of the bitcoins that are currently available everywhere, just the ones in the exchange they are looking to execute the pump and dump in.

While the artificial scarcity will push the price higher naturally, the person who is looking to take advantage of the scenario then also does everything else they can to ensure the price grows as high as possible. This combination of events will then create a scenario where the price is inflated far above what it would otherwise be. Then, when it seems unlikely that the price is going to get any higher, the instigator sells off all of their cryptocurrency, making an extreme profit and tanking the price in the process.

Chapter 3: Bitcoin's Main Competition

Ethereum

Ethereum is the second most popular blockchain-based platform available today. It's cryptocurrency, ether, is primarily used in P2P transactions between individuals as a means for paying for services rendered. Unlike bitcoin, however, there is more to Ethereum than just its cryptocurrency. Ethereum also offers users access to smart contracts as well as the Ethereum Virtual Machine which lets users create their own decentralized apps which operate on the ether cryptocurrency.

Ethereum was conceived of by a programmer associated with Bitcoin by the name of Vitalik Buterin and written about in a whitepaper discussing decentralized applications in fall of 2013. His original pitch was to add a scripting language to bitcoin but his thoughts fell on deaf ears, so he set out on his own to do just that. By the start of 2014, Buterin had his team together and by July 2015, Ethereum as we know it today was ready to launch.

Smart contracts

A big part of what sets Ethereum apart from the pack is its focus on smart contracts of all shapes and sizes. While it may seem complicated, a variation of this type of function is currently available to most checking account users in the form of automated deductions that can be set up either by the user or by a third party with the user's permission. A smart contract works in broadly the same way but from a decentralized position instead of a more centralized alternative. Put another way, a smart contract is the computer code equivalent of the legalese in a contract that stipulates how and when all the little details are carried out.

Versus Bitcoin: While Bitcoin took the world by storm because it was new, Ethereum is currently drawing interest from the professional world due to its excellent implementation of blockchain technology, but also the meaningful ways that smart contracts can change the way business of all types is handled. In fact, in the spring of 2017, a wide swath of blockchain startups, Fortune 500 companies, technology companies and research groups all came together to create an organization known as the Enterprise Ethereum Alliance. Starting with just 30 members, the organization already has more than 100, including companies like Samsung, Intel, Microsoft and JP Morgan.

Outside of smart contracts, there are several other crucial differences between the Bitcoin blockchain and the Ethereum blockchain. One of these differences is the number of blocks that can be created in an hour, bitcoin's blockchain can manage six, while the Ethereum blockchain can manage 300. The disparity is caused by the Ethereum blockchain's GHOST protocol system that causes confirmation to happen much more quickly than it otherwise might. However, it is also known to leave more blocks orphaned, and never confirmed, in the process.

The next relevant point of comparison is the number of units of the cryptocurrency that are available to the public as a whole. Currently, more than 70 percent of all of the bitcoins that are ever going to exist have already been mined, and most of those were mined during the early days of the cryptocurrency when the mining process was much more manageable. On the other hand, only about 40 percent of all of the available ether has been mined which means there is still time to get in on the process if you hurry.

When it comes to making a profit from mining, Bitcoin currently pays miners more, 12.5 bitcoins compared to 5 for Ethereum.

Additionally, while the size of the payment is set to automatically decrease at a set rate, the Ethereum platform is going to soon do away with traditional mining, replacing it with an untested proof of stake model instead.

Transaction rate: The rate that is charged when it comes to the cost of the transaction per user also varies between Bitcoin and Ethereum. Bitcoin always charges a flat rate, which is good for users who regularly complete larger, more complicated transactions. On the other hand, Ethereum charges a variable rate that is more complex, but results in smaller charges for transactions that are less complicated.

Ethereum's payment system is known as the gas system and the amount of gas that a given transaction is going to cost will depend on the required amount of personal storage that the transaction will require, the bandwidth that will be used to get it to the blockchain and its overall level of complexity. The total cost that a transaction will require is then listed for both its gas price and it gas limit.

Think of gas limit as the number of gallons of gasoline that a vehicle's gas tank can hold. The gas price is then the amount that a single gallon of gasoline would cost.This is written as *x* amount of GWEI (price) per gas (unit), e.g., 20 gwei gas price. To fill up your "tank", it takes... - 10 gallons at $2.50 per gallon = $25 - 21000 units of gas at 20 GWEI = 0.00042 ETH. Therefore, the total TX fee will be 0.00042 Ether. Sending tokens will typically take ~50000 gas to ~100000 gas, so the total TX fee increases to 0.001 ETH - 0.002 ETH.

The gas limit can then be thought of as the true limit that the transaction should cost, if any variables were taken to their limit. Knowing this amount is especially useful as it makes it much easier to avoid a scenario where you meant to spend one ether and end up spending 100 instead. Nevertheless, you will want to remember, units of gas that are going to be required for a specific transaction are going to be defined by the way in which the code is executed in the blockchain. If you are looking to decrease the amount of gas that a specific transaction will cost, decreasing the limit is often not the best way to go about doing so. During non-peak transaction hours, 40 GWEI will be enough to get your transaction into the very next block that is verified, while 20 GWEI will be enough to see your transaction is verified within five blocks and 2 GWEI will get your transaction processed within no more than two minutes.

Transaction speeds: The transaction on the Ethereum blockchain are naturally processed much more quickly than those on the Bitcoin blockchain because they use what are known as a Turing Complete Internal Code that allows it to figure out any equation as long as it is given an unlimited amount of time in which to come up with an answer. This code isn't without issues of its own, however, and its existence makes the Ethereum blockchain more vulnerable to attack. So much so that it was used as the means of access for an attack in the summer of 2017 that was so serious it caused the cryptocurrency's blockchain to fork.

Litecoin

The Litecoin cryptocurrency was released in an open-source fashion on GitHub in October of 2011. Created by Charlie Lee, a former Google engineer, who created the cryptocurrency by forking the Bitcoin Core client, decreasing the block generation time, increasing the number of maximum coins, changing the verification method to scrypt and modifying the user interface somewhat. Lee wanted to change the way the blockchain worked that would be, in his opinion, for the better. Specifically, he was already worried about the amount of time that a new transaction was taking to be verified and wanted to decrease it as much as possible.

Also of importance to Lee was altering the way in which the Bitcoin mining algorithm worked to ensure that it was as easy as possible for anyone, anywhere, to get in on the action. Mining litecoins is more memory intensive than mining bitcoins which means that ASIC machines that are converted to mine litecoins can't mine it as efficiently as they can other types of coins. Unfortunately, Lee's code wasn't quite successful enough, and the modern mining machine can still mine litecoins faster than a personal computer.

During its early days, Litecoin didn't do much to remove itself from Bitcoin's shadow. This all changed in the fall of 2013, however, when the price of a unit of litecoin doubled in less than a day. It managed to reach a market cap of $1 billion by the end of that year. Between 2013 and 2017, the market cap of litecoin has more than doubled to nearly $3 billion, equating for approximately 0.5 percent of the total cryptocurrency market cap.

Litecoin reached its current record high of $160 per unit in December of 2017. This is more than $70 higher than the previous high, achieved in September of the same year and was attributed by experts to the overall enthusiasm that affected cryptocurrency prices across the board in the wake of bitcoin reaching nearly $20,00 per unit.

Increased speed: The most interesting aspect of Litecoin is the fact that it is the first of the five biggest cryptocurrencies by market cap to implement what is known as the Segregated Witness (Segwit) technology, which was created as a way of increasing the overall size of the individual blocks that are stored in the blockchain, thus helping more blocks to be verified in an overall shorter period of time. This is done through a process of splitting transactions into two separate segments, removing the portion of the transaction that verifies the sender and moving it to the end of the transaction before counting it as a separate structure.

This allows the primary section of the transaction to retain the data consisting of sender and receiver data, while leaving the new witness structure to take care of any scripts and signatures that the block might contain. The primary section then retains its normal size, minus the missing bits, while the witness section is then compacted down to about 25 percent of its original size.

One of the biggest issues that is currently facing the bitcoin blockchain at the moment is that there is only so much transaction data that can be packed into a single block, of which only one can be created every 10 minutes. This, in turn, severely limits the speed of the entire blockchain as a whole and ultimately, then, the number of users who can successfully use the service at once. This problem is then multiplied even more if there are only a few nodes in the area where the transaction takes place with transaction times easily soaring to an hour or more if this is the case.

Prior to introduction of the Segwit system, many Litecoin exchanges instead simply took place off-chain which means the transaction was completed without waiting for verification to take place. While this allowed for instantaneous transaction verification, it also left every user open to the possibility of double spending attacks and all sorts of other transaction types that affected the validity of the blockchain as a whole.

Furthermore, additional options had been suggested prior to creation of Segwit, though none of them had the benefit of being backwards compatible with the existing blockchain technology which meant that they would have required a hard fork of the Litecoin blockchain before they could be put into action in a serious way. One example of this was known as FlexTans which made each transaction smaller by simply altering the way it was viewed by the system. This would have allowed for significantly more information to be saved per block, but it was not compatible with existing systems.

The other major issue was one of transaction malleability which meant that signed transactions still didn't include all of the relevant transaction data that they could and at one point verifying the sender's signature wasn't even a part of the process. As a result, several different ways of losing, or stealing keys were possible.

Segwit solves these problems, primarily by offering backwards compatibility with a host of Litecoin's legacy blockchain systems. It gets around the limitations to block size that are imposed on Bitcoin by simply changing how the blockchain defines a block. Rather than limiting each block to a million bites of data each,

Litecoin blocks are now limited to one million units. When taken with the subtraction and reduction of the witness portion of each transaction, the end result is that the total amount of information that can be stored in a block increases from 1 MB to 1.8 MB. What's more, it does all of this within the existing protocol for the blockchain which means nothing had to be updated on the node side of things at all.

It also takes into account a longstanding issue that the blockchain has had with malleability as when it removes the signatures form the transaction data it also makes it impossible to change them any more after the fact. The transaction ID is then no longer malleable and thus, much easier to utilize with the lightning network (descried below). This, in turn, helps to increase the overall speed of the blockchain specifically. What's more, it also ensures that writing to the blockchain only needs to occur at the start and the end of every transaction, speeding things up even more.

Lightning network: When it comes to enhancing Litecoin's transaction speeds to the max, the lightning network is its solution to the scalability issues that are, even now, plaguing Bitcoin's blockchain network. While currently only in an alpha state, when it is rolled out in full it will shunt all of the smaller transactions that come across the blockchain to a sidechain, not only allowing them to be completed without having to wait for longer transactions, but actually increasing the speed at which the longer transactions are processed as well as a result.

It is anticipated that this will work by constructing a temporary payment channel to the Litecoin blockchain before them making the designated lightning transaction and then updating the tentative distribution of the channel's funds, only then checking in with the primary blockchain again once the transaction is completed.

This payment channel will then allow the participants to transfer money between one another without needing to first worry about making all of their transactions public for the whole Litecoin blockchain to see. This will then be enforced by making sure that any user who refuses to participate in the new system will receive a penalty. When the channel is first open users will need to specify a set number of their Litecoins to be transferred to the new sidechain.

Scrypt proof of work: The scrypt proof of work model works in a similar fashion to the more common SHA256 hash, just with a slightly different function. It uses a more memory intensive hash to ensure that mining machines were less effective when mining Litecoin than when mining other types of cryptocurrency in hopes of creating a more utilitarian mining process. While this initially meant that a CPU mining approach was more effective with Litecoin than the more standard GPU mining model, the power of the average mining machine has since caught up with this disparity and now the standard GPU model is just as effective with litecoin mining as it is with anything else. Despite the fact that its main purpose failed, however, the simple fact that it is less commonly used means it is less likely to be targeted by hackers than its competitors.

Unfortunately, this proof of work method is not without some issues of its own, starting with the fact that it requires significantly fewer resources for those intent on malicious activities to pull off a successful attack. However, the more common 51 percent attack is actually harder to pull off against the Litecoin blockchain, making its security somewhat of a wash. Current estimates put the requirements to hack the Litecoin blockchain about $400 per megahash per second over a reliable network and would require a hashrate of 30 gigahashes per second. As such, the total estimated equipment to takeover and match the network would be roughly 12 million dollars.

Active creator: Another important, though often overlooked, positive aspect of Litecoin that makes it superior to Bitcoin is the fact that its creator is still around and very active in the cryptocurrency scene. Unlike the Nakamoto alias, who has since gone on to take on an almost folk hero-like persona in the Bitcoin community, Lee remains a very real force behind Litecoin, shaping its growth every step of the way. What's more, as his cryptocurrency runs on the Bitcoin blockchain, it makes him the most active public face of any cryptocurrency that is currently based on that blockchain. Simply having a public face to link to the cryptocurrency, and the blockchain technology that is doing great things on its own, could prove a crucial point in Litecoin's favor when the dominant names in cryptocurrency eventually shake out.

Currently, Lee is hard at work making sure that the Segwit protocol gains popularity among litecoin users. As this adoption is crucial to the eventual rollout of the lightning network as a whole, mass adoption is understandably at the top of his to-do list. The upgrade will go live across the entirety of the chain as soon as 75 percent of all of its users signal that they support the transition. This is significantly less than the 95 percent of all Bitcoin users that will need to agree to the change before it goes live on that network, ensuring that Litecoin will be increasing its speed compared to Bitcoin sooner rather than later.

While this upgrade has already been proven to be beneficial to the community as a whole, one of the great things about cryptocurrency is the fact that its decentralized nature means that no one can enforce their opinion onto anyone else, even if that person is the creator of the cryptocurrency in question. Regardless, simply having the creator of the cryptocurrency around, and vocal, serves to give the community someone to rally around and helps them decide where to place their focus next.

Chapter 4: Getting Started with Bitcoin

2017 was a banner year for Bitcoin, and history books will likely mark it as the year that Bitcoin stopped being a new trend, and started being a going concern. The king of the cryptocurrency started the year at around $1,600 per unit and by the middle of December had climbed to more than $16,000 per unit. This puts it far ahead of any other asset, in terms of yearly growth, by a nearly unimaginable margin. What is especially interesting is just how far the cryptocurrency has come this year, despite the fact that so few people are actually using it, as they would a more traditional currency, with any degree of regularity.

What this likely means, is that, while the current highs might seem inviting, it is unlikely that the current price is a representation of what the market is willing to pay, so much as it is an example of the bubble that surrounds bitcoins growing out of control. This is not to say, of course, that bitcoins are likely to drop back to the price they were at during January 2017 anytime soon, far from it, it is just to point out that every bubble bursts eventually. It is not a question of if, rather than when, and the rapid increase in price (even by bitcoin standards) should lead potential investors to consider what the true market value may be.

While the current round of extreme growth is bound to tire itself out eventually, experts estimate that it will likely take approximately five years before cryptocurrency usage adoption rates reach a point where they can be considered mainstream. When this mass saturation point occurs, then it is likely that the bubble surrounding the cryptocurrency market as a whole will burst for the last time. At this point, a vast majority of the more than 1,000 cryptocurrencies that are currently on the market will ultimately fold, in a scenario that is likely to be reminiscent of the dotcom boom of the late 1990s. As such, if you are planning to get started it is best that you do so sooner rather than later.

Choose a place to keep your bitcoins

Before you can buy any bitcoins, you are going to need a place to keep them. While you can generally leave them in the care of the exchange you end up using (more on that later) this is, at best, a short-term solution as they are more likely going to be targeted by malicious hackers than any one, personal account. Likewise, a wallet is essential because there is no physical version of a bitcoin that you can hold in your hand, which means the wallet that you choose is going to be, literally, your only line of defense when it comes to ensuring that your bitcoins stay where you put them.

Despite the name, you aren't actually going to be keeping any of your bitcoins in your wallet directly. Rather, your wallet is going to hold a pair of keys that are directly associated with your bitcoins, that actually never leave the bitcoin blockchain. There is a public key, which is used to complete bitcoin transactions with other users, as well as a private key which is used to give you full access to your bitcoins and should never be shared with anyone. It is important to keep your key extremely safe as if you lose it you will lose access to all the bitcoins associated with it as well.

There are two categories of bitcoin wallets, cold and hot. Cold wallets are not connected to the internet in anyway which makes them inherently safer than hot wallets, which are connected.

Online wallets: An online wallet is a wallet that stores your bitcoin details in the servers of the company who is running the wallet. If you are working with a particular bitcoin exchange and you have an account with that exchange that stores its own bitcoins, then this is a type of online wallet, though there are several other types as well. Online wallets can be easily accessed from any internet connected device, and require very little effort or personalization to set up. What's more, as they are almost always connected to an ancillary means of generating profit for the company that hosts them, they're almost always free. The biggest downside to this type of wallet is that its server-based storage makes it a much larger target for hackers than any of the other types discussed here.

Software wallet: A software wallet can take the form of a program on your computer or an app on your smartphone or, as is more common these days, both. Depending on the software wallet you choose, you may be able to access your bitcoins even if you don't currently have an active internet connection to verify the details with the blockchain. If this occurs, your balance is then simply updated on the blockchain once you regain internet connectivity. Software wallets are safer than online wallets, especially if you follow the tips discussed in chapter 6.

Hardware wallet: A hardware wallet is a cold wallet which means it never needs to be connected to a computer. It is a small device, little more than a screen connected to a USB drive. Your private key is stored inside the USB drive and encrypted in such a way that the key cannot be removed as a .txt file without your personalized encryption key. While not useful if you are hoping to use your bitcoins on a regular basis, a hardware wallet is a great choice if you are planning to pursue a buy and hold strategy. A common choice is to find a reliable software wallet to use for small amounts of bitcoin that you plan on spending in a reasonable timeframe, and then purchase a hardware wallet for bitcoins that are purchased for a speculative purpose.

Paper wallet: A paper wallet is a novel concept that is both more secure than a traditional hardware wallet, and cheaper as well. A paper wallet stores your private and public key as a pair of QR codes, that, when created in the proper fashion, are virtually untraceable outside of finding the piece of paper that is attached to your private code and accessing the QR code found there directly. In order to create a paper wallet, all you need to do is to visit WalletGenerator.net and click on the GitHub.com link that you find there. From this link you will then download the full WalletGenerator.net website.

With this download completed, you will then want to run as much virus protection software as possible, in order to ensure that there isn't anything hiding, and spying on your computer. Once you receive the clean bill of health, you are going to want to disconnect your computer from the internet by manually pulling the plug. Once you are sure you are really alone, all you need to do is click on the link to the WalletGenerator page found in the downloaded file. Once on the page, click the button to generate a pair of QR codes and then print them off. Finally, make sure you delete the website and any reference to the QR codes from your computer before you reconnect to the internet.

Once this is done, you will have in your possession the only two pieces of paper that can link you to the bitcoin wallet in question, not to mention prove that the wallet in question even exists. All you then need to do is to keep your private key someplace extremely safe, and take a picture of your public key to use on a regular basis.

Brain wallet: A brain wallet is the most secure form of long-term storage for bitcoins possible. While a paper wallet, quite literally, leaves a paper trail, once you erase the creation details from your hard drive, the only way to access a brain wallet will be in your mind. Specifically, if you visit BitAddress.org and then enter a mnemonic phrase that is 12 words, or numbers, long you will be provided with a link to a unique wallet that can only be accessed by typing that phrase into the specific generator you use to create it the first time. Once the page is closed, the link is severed and the only way to gain access to the private key again is to re-enter the phrase. Needless to say, before you add bitcoins to this type of wallet it is important to test yourself and ensure that the phrase you choose isn't going to be something that will easily slip your mind.

Coinbase.com

While you will certainly want to invest the time to find a more reliable long-term wallet, in order to simply get your feet wet trading in bitcoin you will likely want to start by using the Coinbase Copay wallet which is a software wallet that is available, for free, for both iOS and Android phones, as well as the PC. It can be downloaded at Coinbase.com. While like any software wallet it isn't entirely secure, it is more reliable than most and will be plenty secure for your trial purposes, unless you plan on investing heavily right out of the gate.

Once you have downloaded the app in order to get started buying bitcoins, all you need to do is to launch it and then sign up for an account. With this done, you will then find yourself on an account page that should be familiar to you if you have ever used any type of online banking application. From this screen you will be able to buy bitcoins, or sell if you already own them, as well as how you plan to pay for the bitcoins that you want to purchase. Once you chose the number of bitcoins, or a fraction of a bitcoin, you then just need to confirm the transaction and you will be off to the races. You should receive your bitcoins within 30 minutes in most cases, assuming the load on the blockchain isn't more severe than normal. It is important to keep in mind that you won't receive a one to one return on the money you put in as there are fees taken out both for the exchange you are using as well as for the blockchain itself.

If you have been paying attention, then right now you may be confused as nowhere in the preceding paragraph will you find any mention of a cryptocurrency exchange directly. However, the truth of the matter is that in any instance where you find yourself buying bitcoins, unless you are doing some from another person directly, you will be buying them through an exchange. As such, taking the time to look into the exchange that your wallet is affiliated with, not just the wallet itself, is recommended.

Choosing the right exchange

The first thing you are going to need to know about cryptocurrency exchanges is that they are not regulated in the way that more traditional exchanges are. In fact, they aren't regulated at all. While this can certainly lead to scenarios where the exchange you entrusted your money too suddenly vanishes into the night, it also creates numerous benefits that more than make up for the fact that you have to do more research upfront before you get started. What's more, these exchanges are all open 24 hours a day, seven days a week.

In addition to being unregulated, cryptocurrency exchanges are also not directly affiliated with one another which means that you can find differing prices at different exchanges depending on the level of supply and demand that is currently taking place in each. This will even lead to scenarios where you can buy in one exchange and then immediately turn around and sell in another and still make a profit.

In order to get the most up to date information on the current cryptocurrency exchange scene, the first place you are going to want to visit is going to be the subreddit for the Bitcoin community. The people there will be able to point you in the direction of the most trustworthy exchanges, and also make it clear which ones you should stay away from. While a handful of negative comments about a specific exchange can safely be ignored, more than that could indicate a problem. When determining if this is the case, the first thing you are going to want to do is ensure that all of the comments are about different topics, or are generally vague. If they all seem to be focusing on the same topics, however, then you know that you have found an exchange that you should stay away from.

Focus on transparency: Once you have cut the worst of the worst from the list, the next thing you are going to want to do is to pick out the exchanges that have the most positive reviews and then dig a little deeper into them, starting with their overall level of transparency. What this means is that you will need to be sure that any user can access their order book at any time. The order book is a complete listing of all of the transactions that have taken place that have used the exchange as an intermediary. Having access to the order book will help you to ensure that the exchange isn't artificially inflating their numbers. You will also need to know how they verify their operating funds and where those funds are located.

If you are unable to locate all of this information then the exchange in question could be new, small, or otherwise unable to provide this information for a valid reason. Unfortunately, they may also be what is known as a fractional exchange which means you will need to avoid any non-transparent exchange at all costs. A fractional exchange is an exchange that doesn't keep enough operating capital on hand to cover all of its debts. What this means for you is that there is the possibility that you go to withdraw your money from the exchange only to be told that there isn't enough money to pay you back. Needless to say, you will need to do everything in your power to ensure that you don't wind up in this situation.

Overall security: Once you have verified the level of transparency that the exchange in question is working with, the next thing you will need to do is to is to take a closer look at their security. First things first, this means ensuring that they are using a secure protocol which will help keep your private information private. To make sure this is the case, all you need to do is look at the front of the URL for the exchange in question. A secure protocol starts with https, as opposed to just http. Additionally, you are going to want to ensure that there is some type of secondary authentication taking place. This means you will want to be required to do more than just enter a standard password to gain access to your account. While this will likely seem cumbersome at first, it will be more than worth it if you end up keeping your bitcoins where they belong.

Mind the fees: Assuming you find an exchange that meets your requirements so far, the next thing you will need to consider is the type of fees they charge for your standard transaction, as well as what your standard transaction is likely to be. Transaction fees come in two types, fixed and variable. Variable rates are better for those that plan on making a larger number of smaller trades as the amount paid is going to be relative to the size of the transaction taking place. On the other hand, fixed fees are going to be better for those who plan on completing a smaller number of larger transactions, as the fee is going to remain the same no matter what. If you plan on following the buy and hold strategy discussed in a previous chapter, then you will want to find a fixed rate transaction fee exchange.

Similarly, it is important to look for confirmation that the exchange you are considering is locking in the unit price of bitcoin at the time you initiate the transaction, not at the point the transaction is validated. If your exchange doesn't lock prices in until validation has occurred, you run the risk of letting a good deal turn into a bad deal in the interim. Given the extreme level of volatility that bitcoins can experience in a given day, the 10 minutes or so you spend waiting for your transaction to validate may as well be a decade.

Locally sourced: Finally, if at all possible, you are going to want to do your best to ensure the exchange you choose is based in your home country. First and foremost, it will make it easier for you to take advantage of peak trading hours without having to wake up in the middle of the night to do so. Additionally, if you have questions or technical difficulties with the site, choosing a local exchange will make it more likely you won't have to deal with a language barrier when doing so. Even better, however, dealing with a local exchange ensures you the maximum amount of security possible in the off chance that the exchange you are using ends up being fraudulent. This is not to say that you are sure to get your money back, far from it. It is just to say that you have a far greater chance of seeing some type of compensation locally, than you would dealing with a completely foreign exchange.

As a note of caution, it is always important to take the time to ensure the exchange you are looking at deals in your local currency, regardless of whether or not they are actually based in your country. Many exchanges are located in one country and deal exclusively in the currency of another. This is especially true if you are looking to primarily trade in a currency other than the US dollar or the Chinese yen. Missing this crucial piece of information only means you need to add money changing to the list of things you will have to do in order to get started trading bitcoin.

Chapter 5: Investing in Bitcoin

Buying into Bitcoin

While bitcoin has been a quality investment for the past few years, and an investment more profitable than anyone could have expected in 2017, the cryptocurrency market as a whole is still extremely untested overall which means that many of its risks are still very poorly defined, especially when compared to more traditional markets. This naturally makes the highs in the market more dramatic than similar markets, but it also makes the lows much more dramatic as well. There are no guarantees when one is going to become the other, trends can come and go in completely unpredictable patterns that no one has seen before.

As such, in order to ensure that you understand just what you are getting yourself into when it comes to investing in bitcoins, you need to understand how truly volatile they really are. For starters, on its best day, bitcoin's price is still three times more volatile than the price of gold and nearly five times as volatile as the price of any of the stocks on the S&P 500. While this means that you are significantly more likely to lose your investment with bitcoin, you are also far more likely to see significant positive movement in an extremely short period of time. For example, a yearly return of five percent on an S&P stock is considered average. Depending on how bitcoin is moving while you are reading this, it is entirely possible that it could see a five percent increase by the time you are finished reading this book.

Furthermore, while there have been a few notable exceptions, the overall charts for bitcoin for nearly the past decade have only gone up year over year. As such, if you buy into bitcoins with the idea of holding onto your investment for a prolonged period of time you will find that the daily volatility matters far less than its long-term prospects which, for now at least, are still looking strong. Currently about five percent movement per day is considered average for bitcoin, while smaller cryptocurrencies can currently see as much as 15 percent movement per day.

Despite this extreme level of movement, bitcoin is, at its heart, a commodity like any other. While it did essentially create an entirely new class of commodities, they still follow the same rules as base or precious metals. All three groups of commodities are used for both speculative and practical purposes; precious metals are used in the creation of jewelry, base metals are used in various industries and bitcoins are used, ideally, in digital transactions.

With this in mind, it then becomes somewhat easier to determine how the unit price of bitcoin is going to move in the future, all you need to do is determine how the public feels about the service Bitcoin provides. While speculative interest matters more in the short-term, the opinion of the market is what you should ultimately take into consideration for the long-term.

When it comes to real world usage, it is important to keep in mind that Bitcoin's $30 billion-dollar valuation came about based largely on speculative interest. Remember, only about 30 percent of bitcoin transaction made each day are for actual, practical purposes, the rest is speculative. As such, the long-term valuation price is likely to improve moving forward as every day there are more and more people connecting with the bitcoin blockchain for the first time. As this continues to become more and more commonplace, new and improved services are going to be available to consumers that will be easier and easier to use as well, and the induction process will become much easier to manage.

This trend will continue until a point of mass saturation is reached where more people will be using bitcoin, or at least some type of cryptocurrency, than are not, at which point the cryptocurrency market as a whole is likely going to experience a collapse similar to what occurred at the end of the dotcom boom in the late 1990s. This is not to say that all cryptocurrencies will fail at this point, only that a vast majority of those that don't have a viable, non-speculative reason to exist will fade away and only a handful of the strongest, most useful cryptocurrencies will remain. Luckily, based on its dominant market position, unless something changes bitcoin is almost certainly going to be among those that emerge from the ashes.

This mass saturation point is anticipated to occur by approximately 2022. It is important to keep this date in mind when you are investing, as the mass saturation point is also going to result in whatever bubble that is surrounding bitcoin, and all other cryptocurrencies to pop for the last time. What emerges as a result will then be the true price that the market feels bitcoin is worth, and any future bubbles after that point are likely to be less severe. This means that the closer you get to the mass saturation point, the more carefully you are going to need to consider your investment decisions in order to ensure that you don't buy in at a price that is going to be unsustainable in the long-term.

Using the buy and hold strategy: In order to take advantage of the buy and hold strategy, the first thing you are going to want to do is to wait until the price of bitcoin dips as much as you can reasonably expect it to, given its performance around the time that you are thinking of buying in. From there, all you need to do is wait until the price hits an extreme high that seems far above what the actual market value would be if speculator price inflation was removed from the picture. You then sell, wait for a new low and then repeat the process, building up a greater number of bitcoins as a result than what you could have afforded had you simply used your investment capital to buy a round of bitcoins and called it good.

Then, when you have amassed a suitable number of bitcoins, all you need to do is put them in a cold wallet and hold onto them until you are ready to cash them in for the last time. Taking advantage of this process allows you to make full use of an idea known as compounding. The idea behind compounding states that reinvesting your early returns is the best way to maximize your profits in the long run.

To understand just how powerful compounding can be, consider a person in their mid-twenties who wanted to be a millionaire by the time they were 65. In order to make this dream a reality they would need to save an average of $900 per month, every month, between now and the day they retired, assuming they were earning a paltry (for bitcoin) five percent return on their investment per year. However, if this same person waited until they were in their mid-30s to start saving they would need to save about $2,200 each month, and if they waited 20 years to start saving regularly then they would need to save $4,500 each month to see the same result.

While the standard long-term investment plan has to make do with low, yet reliable returns that build on a yearly basis to increase their compounding capital, bitcoin's volatility means that you can likely see the same results as a year or more of compounding via the traditional method in half the time when investing in bitcoin. The additional gains from this type of investing should more than make up for the additional fees that are going to be paid as a result. Currently nearly 70 percent of all bitcoin transactions are made for speculative reasons.

Have a plan: While getting started quickly is the best way to put the full power of compounding to work for you, that doesn't mean you aren't going to want to jump in without first making a plan that is right for you and your long-term goals. This is a crucial step in order to ensure that your investments are helping, as opposed to hindering your maximum investment potential. The first thing you are going to want to keep in mind is that there is no cryptocurrency trading strategy out there that is going to be right for everyone and the first reason that this is the case has to do with risk. Everyone has a different level of risk they are comfortable undertaking when it comes to investment, and trying to overextend when it comes to the level of risk you are comfortable with is a surefire recipe for disaster.

If you are interested in investing in bitcoins, then you are obviously comfortable with risk to some degree, but this doesn't mean there still isn't room for varying levels of commitment to the risk inherent in bitcoin. This will ultimately often come down to what your goals are like when it comes to your investments. If you are risk adverse, that is, as risk adverse as you can be while still believing a bitcoin investment to be a good idea, then starting by making sure that you hold on to your initial investment for as long as possible is a good choice. Alternately, if you are intent on riding the risks of bitcoin to the fullest then you will want to prioritize potential for profit, no matter what. It is important to keep in mind that the only way you will find reward when investing is by taking risks, it is all about finding the right balance between the two for you.

The specifics of the investment plan that you decide on don't matter nearly as much as the fact that after you have decided on a plan that works for you, you make the decision to stick with it unless things change so much that the plan no longer applies. This means considering your goals, not in a vacuum but in the real world so that you can accurately determine what is likely going to stand in your way, so that when the issue does appear you are ready and waiting for it.

Having a plan in place before you put one penny into bitcoins for investment purposes is crucial, especially if you haven't done much investment in the past as otherwise you will find that it is deceptively easy to let your emotions get the better of you. The more readily you can remove your emotions from the equation entirely, the more effectively you will deal with your investments. Forming a plan beforehand and then sticking to it is the best way to ensure that things go as they should in the moment.

In order to make sure that toeing the line when it comes to your plan is as easy as possible, make it a point to never invest more into a given investment that you can realistically afford to lose. If you wouldn't be able to carry on as normal if the money you are investing suddenly caught on fire, then you should be using it in more immediately useful ways instead. The reasons for this should be clear. After all, it is hard to invest objectively if you are more worried about not losing your money, so you can pay your rent than you are in maximizing your investment. Don't forget, if you have more than 10 years before you plan on cashing in your investments, you can afford to take a good deal more risk than you otherwise would.

Know where you are in the market cycle: The market cycle is the name given to a pattern of behavior that all investments go through as they gain and lose favor with the public. The market cycle never changes and it is inescapable. The only variable that comes into play is the timeframe that each portion of it is going to last. While it is a circle, the market cycle is typically said to start at the point where the market as a whole is starting to become optimistic regarding the asset's potential. As a result, the price continues to increase while the market experiences a feeling of euphoria and investors jump onboard assuming things are always going to remain great forever.

From this point, the price typically continues to rise in an unsustainable fashion until the bubble inevitably bursts and prices experience a decline which leads to a brief period of anxiety about the asset's future. This is typically counteracted at this point by a period of denial in which the price might even see a bit of a resurgence. Unfortunately, this is only temporary, and the price will start to drop steadily as the market experiences fear, then depression, and finally panic as the price begins an apparent freefall. Eventually, however, everyone who will have wanted out will have gotten out and a market equilibrium will be restored. Once this happens, investor confidence will slowly begin to rise again, moving from panic, into depression, followed by relief, then hope and finally optimism once more.

Bitcoin has already seen a full rotation of the cycle and, based on the extreme gains at the end of 2017, experts are already predicting that it has passed the optimism stage once more and it is in euphoria once more. The true state of Bitcoin's market cycle will likely be much clearer by spring 2018. The euphoria stage is likely going to last up until the point that mass saturation is reached, so, despite the high price, it is likely that there is still money to be made.

Plan for the long-term: Despite the fact that bitcoins saw almost a $10,000 per-unit jump in the fall of 2017, these results are far from average which means that if you hope to profit from bitcoin, you are going to need to start out with the right mindset. If you make the mistake of starting out with unrealistic expectations, it will only make it more difficult for you to analyze each situation you find yourself in rationally and easier for you to make the mistake of letting your emotions enter the picture.

While the average investment is typically associated with additional risks when viewed through a long-term lens, this is one place where investing in bitcoin is actually going to be less risky than investing in a more traditional investment. This is due to the fact that you can easily divest yourself of your bitcoin holdings at literally any time which means there is no lock-in risk, a serious issue for more cumbersome investments. As such, you can think of investing in bitcoins as putting your money into an extremely risky savings account that has the potential to pay out far more than average.

Traditional Bitcoin mining

If investing in cryptocurrency doesn't sound like it is going to be for you but you still want to make money off this whole cryptocurrency thing sooner rather than later, then cryptocurrency mining might be more your speed. Every cryptocurrency whose blockchain uses the SHA-256 double round hash process when it comes to verifying transactions uses the same basic mining process when it comes to keeping the blockchain safe and secure from external threats. In exchange for mining, miners receive a predetermined amount of the cryptocurrency in question for their help which goes to offsetting costs and also making the entire process worth your time.

A hash function is a type of mathematical function that is also critical to the overall security of the blockchain system. When it comes to cryptocurrency blockchains, this is the encryption system that turns the legible data into what is known as a fixed length output which can be thought of as a sort of unique information fingerprint. There are several different types of hash functions but the most commonly used variant in blockchains is called SHA-256.

In order to verify transactions, miners invest in mining machines, which are specialized computers that can verify transactions far more quickly than a non-specialized alternative. While originally it was possible to mine using a non-specialized mining machine, the complexity of the verification process soon grew too complicated for single machines and that lead to the rise of centralized mining pools where many miners would come together and work on collectively verifying transactions as quickly as possible.

In exchange for the service they provide, bitcoin miners are currently paid 12.5 bitcoins per block mined, though this reward is set to decreases automatically each time 210,000 blocks are mined. This reward is expected to be halved again in 2020. This reward is used to offset the energy and time that is required to validate the blocks in question. Despite, the potential for profit that comes with mining a single block, it is currently becoming difficult for even mining pools to mine blocks quickly enough to make a profit as the energy costs required increase the more difficult the proof of work is to solve.

As such, those who are interested in investing in bitcoin these days typically stick with what is known as cloud mining instead.

Cloud mining

While buying or building your own mining machine, even one that has several GPUs, can be an interesting way to interact with the bitcoin blockchain, hardware mining bitcoin for profit is not nearly as profitable as it once was. Not only is this due to the simple fact that all the easy to mine blocks were taken several years ago, it is due to the fact that mining bitcoins has since become big business. This means that, regardless of the current price of bitcoin, the companies who are mining bitcoin professionally have enough hash rate to ensure that they snatch up a vast majority of all available bitcoin transactions, leaving mining pools and individuals to fight over the scraps.

What this means is that if you hope to see any type of reliable return for your investment into bitcoin mining you need to stop trying to beat the professional organizations and get ready to join them. Through cloud mining, rather than building and purchasing a mining machine, and then having to worry about all the additional costs associated with upkeep, all you need to do is find one of those professional mining organizations, and pay to use some of their mining power.

Cloud mining works by sharing the processing power of one of these bitcoin mining data centers and allowing users to access either some of their hashing power, or even an entire machine, either real or virtual, and then allows the user to keep whatever rewards they earn as a result. To get started with cloud mining, all you need is a bitcoin wallet and a smartphone.

Pros and cons: Cloud mining does come with its own set of additional risks when compared to more traditional types of mining which is why it is important that you fully understand both its pros and cons before you make a decision to commit to this type of investment. Some of the benefits of cloud mining include the fact that you don't need to deal with the daily issues that come with running your own mining machine. This means that you won't need to worry about energy costs, cooling concerns or dealing with the noise that a mining machine running six or seven GPUs can put off, 24 hours a day, 7 days a week. Additionally, your costs are going to be limited to what it costs to join the cloud mining service, as well as whatever they charge per month which means not having to worry about having a GPU burn out or trying to sell an outdated mining system once it ceases to be profitable.

The biggest drawback to this type of service is going to be that you will naturally earn less per transaction that is verified, simply because you are going to have to pay the middle man to run the cloud mining service that you are taking advantage of. It is also important that you carefully read the cloud mining contract that you are provided with to ensure you know just what you are signing up for. There are cloud mining services that require you to commit to a specific length of time, regardless of how much profit you make in that period. Likewise, you may find cloud mining services that shut down if the price of bitcoin drops below a certain point or the cost of electricity rises over a set point. While the specifics might change, forewarned is always going to remain forearmed.

Finally, it is crucial that you do your homework when it comes to deciding on the service to go with as the operating practices of these types of business are typically extremely hard to parse properly. As such, the best place to start your research is going to be the Bitcoin subreddit as it will provide you with the most up to date list of trustworthy cloud mining services. Overall, there are three different types of cloud mining services:

- Hosted mining services lease out entire mining machines and let clients keep whatever is made as a result.
- Virtual hosted machines work the same way, except the machines they lease out are virtually created on various servers.
- Segmented hashrate machines lease out portions of their hashrate and then pay out whatever that hashrate is used to

mine. This is the most common type of cloud mining as of 2017.

Ensure you are going to turn a profit: Before you make a decision regarding one cloud mining service over another, the first thing you will want to do is to determine if the listed rates are going to be enough to allow you to turn a profit. This can be done using a standard mining calculator, though you will have to alter some data to ensure the numbers work out properly.

For starters, the first thing you are going to need to figure out is a substitute for what your monthly electricity costs would be as well as any costs associated with getting your mining machine up and running. What this number is really showing, however, are the overall startup costs of your new investment, plus the ongoing costs that will be accrued as you generate profit, which is the same as the monthly fee you are going to be paying the cloud mining company you are considering.

The conversion process isn't unilaterally one to one, however, especially when it comes to figuring out what to put in when it comes to hardware costs. To determine this amount, you are going to want to look through the details on the cloud mining service and determine what the monthly running costs are going to be. Once you find this number, you can then use it to work out a kilowatt per hour cost which can be done by taking the monthly running cost and dividing by 0.744.

The results from the calculator should then be enough to give you a general idea about what sort of monthly profit you would make by utilizing the cloud mining service in question. While the profits are going to be lower than some other types of bitcoin investment, the buy-in costs are going to be much lower as well which means that as long as you keep your expectations in check, there should still be plenty of room to turn a profit.

Chapter 6: Avoiding Fraud

While this chapter makes every effort to outline all the many ways that scam artists are trying to make money off of bitcoin, it is important to keep in mind that new ways of parting the unwary from their bitcoin are always being developed which means that the older this book becomes, the more likely it will be that there are other means of fraud out there. As such, you are going to want to make an effort to keep up to date on the latest issues to ensure that however you choose to interact with bitcoins, you remain well protected. Regardless, as a general rule of thumb you are going to want to make a concentrated effort to avoid wallets, exchanges and cloud mining services that do not have a well-defined, positive reputation online; anything else will put your money at risk.

Wallets

While cold wallets are secure as long as you follow any relevant safety protocols, hot wallets can be far more dangerous. Fake wallets can be difficult to spot, especially as many will appear to be working normally, while at the same time carrying out some nefarious purpose. In general, you are going to stick to wallets that bitcoin recommends. Even then, however, you will still want to use your best judgement when looking at the website for the wallet in question, starting with the URL.

The first thing you will need to be on the lookout for is a site that doesn't start with a secure URL, which you can determine by looking for the HTTPS. Before you go ahead and download anything, you are also going to want to ensure that you have entered the URL correctly as there are many spyware sites out there that are only a letter or two off from the real thing. Finally, before you go ahead and pull the trigger and hit the download button, take an extra moment to ask yourself if anything seems off about the website. You've been visiting legitimate websites for years. Trust your instincts and if something seems off retreat to safer online waters while you figure out just what is going on.

Assuming the website you downloaded a file from seems as though it is on the level, you are still going to want to run any files you download through two different virus scanners to ensure that you are being as safe as possible. Many fraudulent wallets include key tracers with their software that automatically log everything you type on your computer and transmit it to a third party which means that taking the extra time to scan your files before opening them could save a lot more than just whatever you happened to invest in bitcoin.

If you are thinking about using a wallet that is not directly recommended by Bitcoin, you are going to need to take the time to see what other users have to say about it first. Reddit is the best place to find this type of information, and if you are unable to find out anything on the wallet you are considering, then it is best to refrain until you have a better idea of what you are getting into as opposed to putting your private key at risk.

Exchanges

While most cryptocurrency exchanges at least try to serve their customers as best they can, regardless of whether or not they actually succeed, there are also those out there that are downright predatory. However, with a little practice, the advertisements that you see for various exchanges should be enough to steer you away from those with predatory tendencies. For starters, if you see an advertisement claiming to be an exchange, yet offering to sell you a set number of bitcoins for a set rate, regardless of what they are currently selling for on the open market, then you can be certain that you are looking at an advertisement for a scam.

The truth of the matter is that a bitcoin exchange typically works the same as any other exchange which means that they won't be able to guarantee any price outside of what the market currently dictates bitcoins are worth. When you purchase bitcoins through an exchange, the exchange is actually putting you in touch with a person who is interested in selling the number of bitcoins you are buying. As no seller is going to take less than the current market value for their bitcoins, there is no way for the exchange to guarantee a set number of bitcoins to you at a set rate.

Instead, what is going to happen if you try and take advantage of this too good to be true offer, is that you will be told to send a PayPal transaction to a dummy account and then your bitcoins will never materialize. As such, you should think of this as a red flag and simply walk the other way. Indeed, the other red flag you should be aware of is if you come across an exchange that is offering to buy your cryptocurrency directly through PayPal. This is also not how exchanges work. If you buy into a particular exchange using your cryptocurrency then that cryptocurrency doesn't leave your possession until someone else has paid for it through legitimate channels. These types of scams have you enter your PayPal details and then tell you to send your cryptocurrency to another address, typically found on a QR code so it is especially easy for them to change it when the jig is up.

Phishing scams: If you plan on getting involved with the bitcoin community on more than a superficial level, it is likely that your email address is going to end up on some mailing lists, both good and bad. The bad type of mailing list is typically going to involve a scammer trying to convince you that they are affiliated with some website that you have previously expressed interest in. With this accomplished, they then either send you to a fraudulent website, or ask that you call a phone number to provide the person on the other end with all of your personal data. While initial contact is typically made in these instances by email, popup adds have also been known to be used on occasion. Regardless of how contact is made, responding to it is sure to ruin your day.

If you find yourself facing down an email that seems a little off, the most important thing to remember is to avoid doing whatever it is that the email asks of you. Unfortunately, this is easier said than done, especially if you haven't had much contact with the website in question. The email could even be from an otherwise legitimate source that was hacked to provide the hacker with access to a legitimate email account.

Regardless of the reasons behind it, the first place you are going to want to look to determine authenticity is any URLs that are included in the email. While the link can be written to look like anything, holding your cursor over it will reveal where the link is going to take you, potentially saving you the trouble of having to look more closely at its contents. If you ever feel as though you are unsure if a specific email is legitimate, the first thing you are going to want to do is contact the website in question through official channels, never through any contact information provided in the email directly. Contacting the company directly is a surefire way to ensure that everything is as it should be.

If you feel as though you are dealing with this issue on a regular basis, then you may need to take more care when it comes to deciding which websites you are going to want to visit online. The most common way of making yourself known to the person operating a phishing scam is by searching for something on Google and then clicking the very first link that comes up. The first few links on any search are going to be advertisements, and these advertisements can easily lead to dangerous websites. You can negate this risk entirely by simply knowing where you are going online before you get there.

Cloud mining services

When it comes time for you to seriously look into choosing a cloud mining service, it addition to working out what the costs will be, it is important that you dig a little deeper and ensure that they are actually on the level. While there is the potential for fraud across the cryptocurrency space, the risk associated with cloud mining services is much greater, simply because it can be easy to create a purely fraudulent system that continues to appear effective as long as new marks continue buying into it.

The way it works is, these types of scams set up what appears to be a fully-functional cloud mining service and attract an initial round of interest at what appears to be an extremely competitive rate. Then, it uses a portion of the fees that it is collecting each month to pay out other users. This process can work successfully for years, as long as the cloud mining service can keep bringing in enough new customers that older customers don't figure out what's going on.

While this might seem fairly benign, the reason you need to carefully vet your cloud mining service is because these sorts of scams can never keep going indefinitely. Instead, they are bound to eventually start failing to bring in new clients at a rate that is enough to keep all of the old clients paid. A missed payment here or there will eventually lead to a complete cessation of payments all together as the owner of the scam closes up shop, only to reopen somewhere else online using a different name.

Avoid referrals: One of the clearest indicators that something isn't right about a cloud mining service that you have chosen is if they seem to put an undo emphasis on getting their clients to refer other people. If a cloud mining company is on the level then they should be able to find new clients on their own, without constantly pestering their clients to do their job for them. You will also be able to easily tell if the company you are looking into is a scam if you can find proof that they have cut their prices several times over the past year. The owners of these scams care about putting as many people into the system as possible, regardless of what each pay, and price cuts are a great way to address concerns of flagging interest.

Look into the specifics: In addition to keeping an eye out for referrals, you are going to want to dig into the specifics of what the company is offering as thoroughly as possible. The best place to start is with the total amount of hash rate the pool has available to them. A serious red flag is going to be any company that asserts they have an unlimited, or nearly unlimited hash rate. A true cloud mining company will know exactly what hash rate any one of their servers can pull, and will also have a hard time adding to their current rate. The cost and difficulty typically associated with adding a new server the size and scope that most cloud mining companies deal with is not insignificant, and the machines need to be built to spec which takes an unavoidable amount of time.

What all this means is that any company that is claiming that they have an unlimited hash rate is lying, no two ways around it. While this doesn't necessarily mean that they are completely fraudulent, it certainly means you don't want to be dealing with them. Even if the company in question doesn't directly state that they have an unlimited hash rate, it is still important to request as many details about their infrastructure as possible. This includes pictures of both their facilities and their servers, which you should then run through a Google image search to ensure they aren't stock photos. Regardless of what response you may get to the contrary, this is a perfectly reasonable request and anything other than compliance will indicate the company in question is up to something.

ASIC seal of approval: Finally, one of the best signs that a cloud mining company is a fraud is if they don't provide either the ASIC seal of approval or a written endorsement from the company. ASIC is the name in specialized bitcoin mining equipment and if the company that you are considering is mining bitcoins on a professional level then the odds that they use ASIC are incredibly high. Additionally, ASIC likes providing this type of verification for websites as it is good publicity for their brand while also associating the name with quality. What this means is that if you can't find the ASIC logo somewhere on the site, then there has to be a reason why, and it likely isn't going to be doing you any favors.

Chapter 7: Tips for Success

Don't be afraid to diversify: While bitcoin is currently proving to be a surprisingly robust investment, especially in 2017, once you have set up your initial investment to the point that you only need to check on it from time to time to ensure things are continuing to go according to plan, it may be time to check and see what else is out there. As a general rule, the more diversified your investments are the better, and experts recommend that your long-term investments are split between two and five different places as opposed to going all in on just one investment. Doing otherwise can cause you to lose everything from a single round of extremely negative volatility and is not recommended.

This is where creating an investment portfolio comes into play and why it is something that everyone should consider at some point, regardless of their overall investment strategy. Diversification is crucial to protecting your investment in the long-term, especially with investments such as bitcoins which experience such a high degree of volatility. When it comes to considering other cryptocurrencies to diversify into, you're in luck, there are more than 1,000 to choose from. In order to limit your search to a reasonable amount, you are going to want to look into cheaper cryptocurrencies that you can easily invest heavily into, without putting out too much additional capital.

Just because a cryptocurrency is cheap doesn't mean you aren't still going to want to do your research before investing heavily. Remember, ensuring that the cryptocurrency that you are considering is going to actually add value to the marketplace is key to its eventual success. There is very little to be gained from investing in a cryptocurrency that is purely speculative, no matter how cheap it may be at the moment.

A good example of this as of the end of 2017 is lumens. Trading at just more than 1 cent per unit, it is being targeted specifically at those in the third world that traditionally have had a difficult time gaining access to standard banking services. What's more, it is being backed heavily by the founder of the first ever bitcoin exchange, Mt. Gox. A low cost, high potential for value cryptocurrency such as this makes a perfect counterbalance to bitcoin. Who knows, five years from now it could be sitting at $100 a share and you could be looking at a ten-thousand percent return on your investment.

Keep abreast of current trends: Just because the most practical bitcoin investment strategy involves buying as many bitcoins as possible and holding on tight, doesn't mean that you don't need to keep abreast of what is going on in the world of bitcoin on a regular basis. While bitcoins are known for pricing peaks and valleys, this doesn't mean you are always going to ride out every low blindly without looking into the causes behind it.

As such, you are going to want to pay enough attention to the marketplace to know when a little rockiness represents just a bump in the road and when it represents a serious downturn that might represent a burst speculator bubble.

Determining if the right choice is to stick it out or cut and run isn't going to be cut and dry; rather, it will depend on several personal factors. When you think a serious downturn is coming you will want to consider your timeline, your tolerance for risk, what your trading plan says to do and how accurate it appears to still be based on everything else that is currently taking place.

Don't forget that Bitcoin is still new: While so much industry has grown up around cryptocurrency in general between 2008 and 2017, it is important to keep in mind that it is a technology that is very much still in an infant state. For example, consider what the average automobile looked like 10 years after Henry Ford started mass producing them. While the people at the time were likely certain that things could never get any better, history has decidedly proven them wrong. All this is to say that there is still more about cryptocurrency that we don't know than what we do, which means that change could literally be around the corner at any time.

As such, it is important to go into any investment with the mindset that things could be ready to change and at any time, which means you need to be ready to make snap decisions, when needed. This, in turn, means that you are likely going to need to understand not just where blockchain is at in the moment, but where it is likely going as well. Keeping an eye on the more speculative technological edge of cryptocurrency is sure to pay off in the long run.

Additionally, this means having the right expectations for your investments in general. While the price is known to jump dramatically from time to time, this is assuredly the exception rather than a rule. As such, in order to pull off the buy and hold strategy successfully, you will need to be careful to avoid expecting too much, too soon. Remember, even if you buy into bitcoin and see a relatively paltry 15 percent return your first year, that is still significantly better than what any other speculative form of investment can expect.

Remember, formulate a plan and stick to the plan up until the point that the situation changes so much that your plan no longer makes sense. Your plan should have been created when you were at your most composed and level headed, changing it up without going through as much work as you did when you created it is sure to leave you open to risks that you would be aware of if you took the time to keep yourself from acting rashly in the moment.

Get started on the right foot: In order to start investing in bitcoin successfully, it is important to maximize your potential investment capital early on, to fully take advantage of any positive volatility that takes place while you are holding it. This means that while you will certainly make a profit if you put a few hundred dollars into bitcoin, the profit you see when it increases will be limited to the total amount you are holding overall. This is why starting with the right amount of trading capital for the cryptocurrency you are considering is so important. For example, at nearly $20,000 per unit, a $200 investment in bitcoin will barely buy you one-hundredth of a bitcoin which means that each time the price of bitcoin increases by $1,000, you earn about $10. Meanwhile, for that same $200, if you bought into lumens you could acquire about 10,000, and if they increased by $1,000 you would be a millionaire.

While obviously there is much about bitcoins that makes them superior to lumens, the point is that having the right amount of available capital to ensure that your efforts are properly rewarded is crucial to being successful in the long run. Additionally, it is important to start off with plenty of trading capital to help you keep any potential losses in perspective. For example, if you invest $100 in Bitcoin and the price immediately drops by $500, then the emotional gut punch that this generates, regardless of the fact that it is ultimately meaningless in the long-term, is that it will be much more difficult to keep your emotions in check than it would otherwise be. This, in turn, will make it more likely for you to start making decisions on tilt, which will most likely result in you losing even more money in the long run.

Don't worry about getting the best price possible: It was previously noted that the trends that bitcoin pricing will experience are more difficult to predict than those of its more traditional speculative investing counterparts. This is largely due to the fact that there is very limited historical data to consult when it comes to bitcoin pricing, especially in the extreme highs it was experiencing at the end of 2017. This fact is only magnified by the extreme volatility that is already in play which means that trends that start off strong in the morning could be completely gone 20 minutes later.

This, in turn, means that if you try and wait for the peak pricing momentum to make your move, you could often find yourself overshooting and ending up with a lower price as a result. This does not, of course, mean that it is best to simply throw money into the market whenever the mood strikes you and hope for the best. Rather, it simply means that with careful planning you can ensure that it works out in your favor instead.

This means you will always want to take a measured approach to bitcoin investing and only put more money into bitcoin when the market indicates that it is a good time to do so. This same care should be given to the time you plan on placing your bitcoins from the market as you never know when extreme fluctuations may occur, or when they will end once they begin. Remember, almost getting the best possible price is better than getting a lower price that you had a chance to move on and actively chose against. All told, the best choice is going to be sticking to one side of markets that are range bound as this will almost always lead to greater profits overall.

Always know when you will be getting out: Just because the most profitable way to invest in bitcoin at the moment is through the utilization of the buy and hold, this doesn't mean that you shouldn't also have an exit plan in mind that you give as much thought to as you do to your entry plan. This is a step that new investors commonly avoid without even really thinking about it, though this likely only happens once as the losses incurred make it a lesson that is easy to remember. As such, they often find themselves either getting out too early or too late, missing out on easy potential profits as a result.

If you find that you are having difficulty finding the perfect time to exit a particular investment, the best place to start is by adding more technical specificity to your exit plan. Once you add these to the mix you will then want to make sure you do not blindly follow them and instead make sure that you are changing them up on a regular basis in order to make sure that your plan is in line with the current market environment.

Don't forget that the market doesn't care about you: While it will certainly seem otherwise sometimes, it is important to keep in mind that, to the market, you are not a beautiful and unique snowflake which means it is always going to do just what it wants to do regardless of what you might have to say about the matter. While everyone understands this intellectually, it can be a different concept for new investors to understand emotionally, especially when a sure thing turns into a serious loss at the last possible minute. When something like this occurs, it is important to remind yourself that you are focusing on the long-term and that only the end results matter, what happens in the middle is just filler.

One thing that is always going to remain constant in these situations is the fact that you will always end up losing out if you let the times when you lose out on an apparent sure thing cause you to doubt yourself and your plan. This is a surefire way to end up on tilt and follow a single bad decision with many more, each of which will be more difficult to come back from than the last. Regardless of what's at stake, holding onto a position in an effort to ensure things turn around properly, after it is clear that things are not going to right themselves, is akin to throwing good money after bad which is why you should always place all your focus on the numbers and let everything else speak for itself.

Making a concentrated effort to control your ego as well as your self-esteem will also go a long way towards making it easier for you to focus on the price action that is actually taking place in a given scenario, practically to the exclusion of everything else around you. This will help to ensure that you can more easily break free of negative mental tracks that making even the likelihood of breaking even as a profitable means of moving forward. You will likely also notice an overall improvement in your results if you wait to determine if a given choice ends up being a success or failure until after everything has played out completely.

Don't feel the need to follow the crowd: Just because there is some currently hot trend that is burning up the bitcoin charts doesn't mean that it is going to successfully sit around for long enough that it will be profitable for you. The bitcoin market is far more prone to fluctuations of all type than any other type of security which means that doing so is a surefire way to end up throwing money out of the window. Before you make any move, you are going to want to look at it from every possible angle to help you to put the current movement in context and allow you to make the best decision possible based on the information that is currently available to you.

Additionally, while every bitcoin investor is going to have their own opinions when it comes time to the best time to get into or get out of a given investment, or what given pricing indicators really mean, those who have experience in investment have learned to largely ignore the opinions of others in favor of what works for them. In order to ensure you make a profit from bitcoin, you need to be clear on your entry and exit points along with the math that you used to determine both of these points. This means you are going to want to remain a neutral observer at all times when it comes to the economic and political events that could affect the unit price of bitcoins. If you get caught up in the moment, you could easily end up focusing on the issue, and not on how it is going to affect your bitcoin investment.

Don't focus on the wrong things: When you first get started investing in bitcoin, it can be easy to get so focused on one particular aspect of your investment plan that it becomes easy to forget that nothing that you do when it comes to bitcoin is going to exist in a vacuum. Not keeping this fact at the forefront of your mind is a surefire way to subject yourself to losses that are otherwise completely preventable. Instead, the more worthwhile approach is going to be to take a macro view of any of the trades that you are considering as a way of minimizing any general derivatives.

While these derivatives are going to be vital when it comes to making sure that market forces are all moving in the right direction before you go ahead and make a move, it is important to not end up taking so much of a macro view that you lose sight of the things that matter most in the short-term, as well as the long-term. Remember, a mixed micro and macro view is surely going to yield the best results.

Don't be afraid to pull the trigger: While at times it will seem as though the only thing you are doing when it comes to investing in bitcoin is doing research, it is important to not get so caught up in finding the right moment that you don't act on it when it actually arrives. This is especially common with new traders who feel the pressure of success more acutely than experienced traders, which can make it difficult for them to trust in themselves and make the decision to enter an investment, regardless of what the consequences might be. While this fear is perfectly normal, the only way to master it is to do that which you are afraid of. After you have made a few successful investments you will find that the entire process becomes much more manageable.

On the contrary, it is important to also make sure that you don't get so caught up in the idea of missing out on the right moment that you end up jumping in to early and missing out on potential profit in the process. Moving too early or too late can be just as harmful as not moving at all, possibly more so. In fact, some experts suggest that investors picking the right time to move forward with a given investment at the wrong time miss out on as much as 10 million dollars each day. This doesn't mean you need to wait until everything's perfect, it just means you are going to want to find the best entry point you can and then let the chips fall where they may.

In order to ensure that things work out as planned, you are going to want to understand the trend that you are keeping track of, along with the relative strength of the market as a whole as well. The most important thing you can do overall, however, is never moving on either a tip from a friend, or a personal hunch, without first taking the time to do the required research beforehand. It is far better to miss out on something because you took the time to do your homework, then it is to invest heavily at the wrong time because you didn't know what you were getting into.

Never average down: While no one ever starts off planning on averaging downward, new traders frequently get caught in the trap of doing so now and again simply because they don't first stop and plan to ensure it doesn't have a chance to occur in the first place. The truth of the matter is that the resources that you are going to spend by remaining attached to a weak position that is not gaining strength, is often going to end up costing you more that if you had just ended the position when things went south initially almost every time. There is almost always going to be a better use for the funds in question than simply sitting around and waiting for things to creep back to their starting point, and if you hope to maximize your profit in the long term then you need to always be thinking about how to best ensure your money is working for you, right now.

Additionally, it is important to keep in mind that if a given investment doesn't work out, that means your next endeavor needs to be even more successful, right out of the gate, just to ensure that you break even. If you find yourself in a seemingly never-ending cycle of averaging down, especially if your investment capital wasn't terribly strong to being with, then it might not take much to cause you to end up back where you started.

Pay more attention to risk and reward: It should go without saying that both risk and reward play a key role in every trade. It is important to avoid the mistake of thinking that they are equals, however, as nothing could be further from the truth and if you fail to take what makes them different into account them you will likely find yourself making the wrong moves without even being aware of what you are doing. It is important to have a clear idea of what you expect to gain from your investment, both in the short and the long-term, in order to ensure that things are proceeding apace. It is important to have a firm risk/reward ratio in mind and stick with it, in order to avoid depleting your investment capital too quickly with poorly timed initial investments.

Conclusion

Thank you for making it through to the end of *Bitcoin Investment Basics - Tips for Success (Mastering Bitcoin for Starters)*, let's hope it was informative and able to provide you with all of the tools you need to achieve your goals, whatever it is that they may be. Just because you've finished this book, however, doesn't mean there is nothing left to learn on the topic. Expanding your horizons is the only way to find the mastery you seek.

Perhaps more than any other hot button issue of the time, successfully investing in Bitcoins means dedicating yourself to becoming a lifelong learner. New technologies, investment strategies and price-changing events are coming to light every day which means that if you are content to rest on your laurels there is a very real chance that you will miss something that will affect your investments in a serious way. Remember, when it comes to becoming an expert on Bitcoin, the journey is a marathon, not a sprint, slow and steady wins the race.

While there are plenty of different ways to make money from Bitcoin, the most important thing you need to keep in mind is that the clock is ticking, which means that if you are going to get started, the sooner the better. It is entirely possible that an investment opportunity of this magnitude will not come around in your lifetime again, if you don't take advantage of it you may quite literally never get another chance. Consider your options, make a plan and stick with it and you will be well on your way to achieving your bitcoin investment goals.

Finally, if you found this book useful in any way, a review on Amazon is always appreciated!

Thank you and good luck!

Blockchain

The Ultimate Guide to
Understanding the Technology
Behind Bitcoin and
Cryptocurrency (Including
Blockchain Wallet, Mining,
Bitcoin, Ethereum, Litecoin,
Ripple, Dash and Smart Contracts)

Leon Watson

including specific information will be considered an illegal act irrespective of if it is done electronically or in print. This extends to creating a secondary or tertiary copy of the work or a recorded copy and is only allowed with express written consent from the Publisher. All additional rights reserved.

The information in the following pages is broadly considered to be a truthful and accurate account of facts and as such any inattention, use or misuse of the information in question by the reader will render any resulting actions solely under their purview. There are no scenarios in which the publisher or the original author of this work can be in any fashion deemed liable for any hardship or damages that may befall them after undertaking information described herein.

Additionally, the information in the following pages is intended only for informational purposes and should thus be thought of as universal. As befitting its nature, it is presented without assurance regarding its prolonged validity or interim quality. Trademarks that are mentioned are done without written consent and can in no way be considered an endorsement from the trademark holder.

TABLE OF CONTENTS

x

Introduction

Congratulations on downloading your personal copy of *Blockchain: The Ultimate Guide to Understanding the Technology Behind Bitcoin and Cryptocurrency (Including Blockchain Wallet, Mining, Bitcoin, Ethereum, Litecoin, Ripple, Dash and Smart Contracts).* Thank you for doing so.

As more cryptocurrencies, such as Bitcoin, start gaining popularity all over the world, a considerable amount of attention from media outlets will bring the term blockchain out of obscurity. In the financial and tech worlds, blockchain has become somewhat of a buzzword.

With all this hype surrounding blockchain, what does it actually mean? What is blockchain? What can you do with it? Why is it important? The media often doesn't answer these questions, but that's what this book is here to do.

This book isn't here to plumb the depths of the math and code wizardry that runs blockchain. Instead, it's here to serve as an introduction to the concept of blockchain technology.

There are plenty of books on this subject on the market, thanks again for choosing this one! Every effort was made to ensure it is full of as much useful information as possible. Please enjoy!

Chapter 1: A Brief History of Central Banking

A simple definition of central banking is an authority that is responsible for the policies that have an effect on a country's credit and money supply. A bank can use monetary policy tools like changes in reserve requirement, discount window lending, and open market operations to change the monetary base and short-term interest rates to gain policy goals.

There are three goals of the modern monetary policy. The most important one is price stability. This means banks need to maintain a low inflation rate. The second one is having an economy that is stable. This can be seen in economic growth and high employment rates. The third one is having financial stability. For this, you need to have a smooth running system of payments to prevent a financial crisis.

The beginning of central banking can be traced back to the 17th century. The first recognized central bank was the Swedish Riksbank. This was founded in 1668 as a stock bank and was meant to give the government funds and a place to make exchanges, securities, payments, and transactions. In 1694, the Bank of England became the central bank of the time. It was created as a stock company to buy government debt. Later on, other banks were founded for the same purposes. Some were created to help with monetary disarray. In 1800, Banque de France was founded by Napoleon to help the currency stabilize after paper money was inflated during the French Revolution. It also helped with government finance.

Early banks gave out private notes that could be used as currency. They held the monopoly over these notes. The early banks funded the government's debt.

Private entities also engaged in banking activities. Since these banks held deposits for other banks, they basically became banks for the bankers. They facilitated transactions between two or more banks or provided other services. They were the storehouse for many banks within the banking system since they had large reserves and a network of other banks. All of these things let them become the last resort when faced with a financial crisis. They were willing to give out emergency cash to other banks if they were facing financial distress.

The Federal Reserve System is part of the central banks that were founded at the beginning of the 20th century. These banks were built to consolidate the different types of currency people used and to give some needed financial stability. Most were founded to handle the gold standard that most countries were initially involved with.

The gold standard that was around until about 1914 was how each country defined their currency. They held huge reserves of gold on hand so that notes could be changed into gold, as needed. When reserves began to decline due to a deficit of payments or other adverse circumstances, they would raise their rates or the interest rates that they lent to other banks. This would cause the interest to go up in general, and thus attract investment from foreign countries and bring even more gold back into their country.

Central banks stuck to the rule of the gold standard by maintaining gold's convertibility. This served as their economy's anchor. In other words, how much money the bank could supply was determined by how much gold they held in their reserve. This would also determine the price of gold, since the price level was tied to a commodity whose value was figured by the force of the market. The expectations about the price level's future were also tied to it. These early banks were committed to the stability of price. They didn't worry about the

9

stability of the true economy since their obligations caused them to stick to the gold standard.

Centrals banks during this time were also lenders in times of stress. When wars, railroad defaults, and/or bad harvests occurred, people scrambled to try and convert their deposits into cash. This lesson was learned early in the 19th century by the Bank of England because they always responded to these times of panic.

The banks would try to protect their gold reserves first and would turn away people who were in need. This caused many panics in 1825, 1837, 1847, and 1957. This led to the Bank being severely criticized. The Bank finally adopted a responsibility doctrine, that was proposed by Walter Bagehot, an economic writer of the time. He suggested the Bank give its private funds to the public. When Parliament enacted the Reform Act of 1867, the Bank started following "Bagehot's Rule". This led to Banks freely lending provided a person offered any collateral that was worth money but with a penalty rate to prevent people from defaulting. The bank had learned its lesson. There were no more financial crises in England for almost 150 years after the year of 1866. The country did not have another financial crisis until August 2007.

The United States has had more interesting experiences. There were two central banks in the early 1800s. The bank of the United States from 1791 to 1811 and the Bank of the United States from 1816 to 1836. Both had been set up just like the Bank of England. However,

Americans were not like the British, and they didn't trust any type of financial power whatsoever, especially central banks. Therefore, the bank's charters were never renewed.

There was an 80-year span faced with financial instability from 1781 to 1862. During the span of years from 1836 to the beginning of the Civil War, was known as the Free Banking Era. During this time, only state-chartered banks existed and states would let anyone have money without any regulations. During this time, banks would fail, and many panics occurred. Their payment system was very inefficient. They had thousands of bank notes and counterfeit notes in circulation. The U. S. government responded to this by creating the national banking system in the middle of the Civil War. This improved the payment systems because it provided a single currency that was based on national bank notes. It didn't provide last resort lending and experienced several banking panics.

A crisis in 1907 led to the Federal Reserve being created in 1913. Its main goal was to provide an elastic and uniform currency. A currency that would stand up to the secular, cyclical, and seasonal movement within the economy and would serve as a central bank.

Central banks didn't worry about the economy's stability before 1914. However, after World War I this changed. The banks started worrying about price levels, real activity, and employment. This showed a change within the political economies of most countries. Migration restriction was being put in place,

Labor movements were beginning to rise, and suffrage was growing. The Federal Bank started focusing on internal and external stability. This meant they would be watching the gold reserves since the United States was still using the gold standard. They would also be watching employment, output, and prices. If the gold standard stood the test of time, their external goals would dominate.

Their monetary policy would lead to problems in the 1920s and 30s. The Federal Bank used a principle that was called the "real bills doctrine" to manage the nation's money. This doctrine stated that the economy would supply the amount of money it needed if the Banks only gave funds when banks could provide self-liquidating paper as collateral. One consequence of this doctrine was that the

Federal Bank should give money to finance stocks. This is why it followed a policy to balance out the boom on Wall Street. This policy caused a recession in August of 1929 that led to the stock market crash in October. During all these banking panics between the years of 1930 and 1933, the Federal Bank didn't respond like a central bank. The supply of money collapsed, and what followed was a massive deflation and then the Great Depression. The Federal Bank responded incorrectly since the doctrine caused it to think the short-term interest rates were a sign of easing of money. They thought that banks didn't need any funds since other banks weren't asking for money.

Following the Great Depression, the U. S. government reorganized the Federal Reserve.

The Banking Acts of 1933 and 1935 changed the power from the Banks to the Board of Governors. This made the Federal Bank dependent on the Treasury. The Federal Bank got its independence back in 1951 when it started following a policy under the direction of William McChesney Martin. This policy was successful in the 1950s in eliminating some recessions and keeping inflation low.

In 1944, the US and other countries became part of the Bretton Woods System. This system set the price of gold at $35 an ounce, and other countries attached themselves to the dollar. The gold link might have carried some credibility as an anchor and kept inflation low.

When the Federal Banks started following a better stabilization policy, the picture changed greatly in the 1960s. During this time, its priorities changed from keeping inflation low to high employment. The shift in policy was caused by inflation pressures from the 1960s and 1970s. What caused this Great Inflation is still being worked out. This period is known as the lowest point in banking history. When the U.S. removed the dollar from the gold standard in 1971, the restraining influence of this anchor disappeared, and during the next 20 years, inflation took off.

Inflation ended due to Paul Volcker's tenure as Chairman of the Federal Bank during the years of 1979 to 1982. This involved raising the interest rates to double digits. What became known as the Volker shock caused a sharp recession and broke high inflation expectations. During the next decades, there was a significant decline in inflation. It has continued to stay low to this day. In the early 1990s, the Federal Bank began targeting inflation. The policy tried to follow the gold standard. This made the public think that the Federal Bank was committed to keeping low inflation.

The main force in central banking's history has been its independence. The beginning banks were independent and private. They needed the government to stay operating but could choose their policies and tools. They were only constrained by how convertible gold was. During the 1900s, many of the central banks were nationalized and lost their independence. The policies were now dictated by authorities. The Federal Banks got its independence back after 1951. However, Independence is not a guarantee. They are required to report to

Congress, who has the power to change the Federal Reserve Act. Other banks didn't get their independence back until during the 1990s.

Chapter 2: Blockchain Technology

Blockchain is a clever and original invention of Satoshi Nakamoto – a pseudonym of a person or a group of people. But since its inception, it has grown to something more, and one of the biggest questions that people ask is: what exactly is blockchain?

By letting digital information be shared, but not replicated, blockchain made the internet a new backbone. It was originally created for Bitcoin, a digital currency, but the tech community had found other possible uses for this technology.

A lot of people refer to Bitcoin as 'digital gold,' and probably for a good reason. So far, the market capitalization of bitcoin is nearing 200 billion USD. Blockchains are also able to create other digital value. Just like with your car or the internet, you don't have to learn how the blockchain works in order to use it. However, it doesn't hurt to have a basic understanding of this technology. By knowing the basics of this technology, you will understand why it is considered significant and revolutionary.

Distributed Database

Imagine a spreadsheet duplicated over a thousand times throughout a computer network. Then visualize that the network was made to update the spreadsheet regularly. That's blockchain. Basic, right?

Blockchain houses information that exists as a shared database. There is no centralized form of the information that a hacker can corrupt. Anybody on the internet can access the data because it is hosted by millions of computers at the same time.

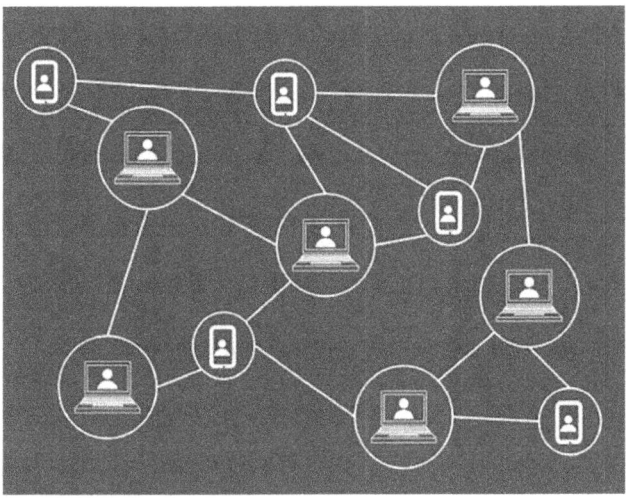

Like the internet, blockchain is built with robustness. Since there are stored blocks of identical information all throughout the network, no single person can control the blockchain and there is no single failure point.

Bitcoin was created in 2008, and since then the Bitcoin blockchain has worked without any major disruptions. The problems that *have* occurred with Bitcoin are because of mismanagement or hacking. Basically, the problems came from human errors and bad intention, not from flaws in its concepts. The internet has been durable for nearly 30 years. That's an achievement that bodes well for the continuous development of blockchain.

Being in a constant state of consensus, blockchain continuously checks itself every 10 minutes. The blockchain network reconciles each transaction in 10-minute interludes.

Every transaction group is called a block. There are two properties that come from this:

1. Transparency. The data is public because the data is inserted in the network as a whole.
2. It is not able to be corrupted. A huge amount of computing power is needed to change any information in the blockchain to supersede the complete network.

We can conclude that it may be possible, but in actual practice, it's not very likely. If you control the system to get Bitcoins, it would also end up destroying their value.

Made Up of Nodes

There are networks of computing nodes that make up the blockchain. Together these nodes make a robust second-level network, a completely different way for the internet to work.

Each node works as an administrator for the blockchain. Each can join the network voluntarily; this makes the network decentralized. However, every one of them has an incentive for network participation: the possibility of getting Bitcoins.

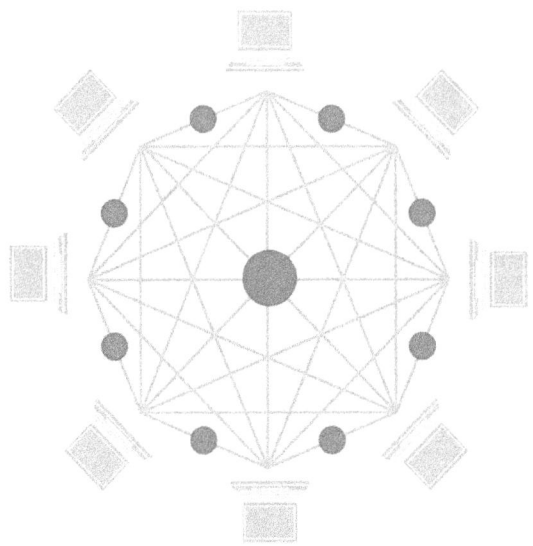

Many believe that nodes mine Bitcoin, but this is a misnomer. In actuality, every one of them is competing to try and get Bitcoins by solving complex computations puzzles. Bitcoin was the main reason why blockchain was created. Or so that's what it seemed. Turns out, Bitcoin is only the *first* of the several different technology applications.

There are around 700 cryptocurrencies that are currently available. There are also other possible modifications of the original blockchain that are in development or currently active.

Decentralization

Blockchain was designed to be a decentralized technology. That means anything that will happen on the blockchain will be a function of the network in its entirety. Several important implications come from this. Through coming up with a new method in verifying the transactions, some aspects in traditional commerce may now be unnecessary.

Stock market trades can become nearly synchronous on the blockchain. It can also make record keeping, such as land registry, completely public. Decentralization is already a part of it.

A global computer network jointly controls the database that houses all of Bitcoin's transactions using this technology. This means that Bitcoin is controlled by its own network – not by a single authority. Since the network is decentralized, it operates on a peer-to-peer (P2P) basis. The different forms of mass collaboration that make this possible are only now beginning to be looked at.

You don't need complex knowledge about blockchain to use it. Currently, finance is one of the strongest uses for blockchain. The blockchain can possibly remove the mediators for a lot of transactions. The public got access to personal computing with the creation of GUI, graphical user interface, which turned into a 'desktop.' The most common GUI that was created for blockchain is the 'wallet' applications. They can be used to purchase online items with Bitcoin. They can also be used to store Bitcoins as well as other digital currencies.

Sharing Economy

With businesses like Airbnb and Uber growing, there is no doubt that the sharing economy has proven successful. Presently, users that are in need of a ride have to depend on services such as Uber. By using peer-to-peer payments, blockchain provides direct and effective transaction between parties.

A good example of this is OpenBazaar. They use blockchain to make a peer-to-peer version of eBay. If you download the app onto a computing device, you will be able to transact with OpenBazaar vendors without having to pay a transaction fee. The fact that it doesn't have any rules means that the reputation of the participants will be more essential to the business interactions than with eBay.

Governance

With results becoming publicly accessible and transparent, elections or other poll taking events can become completely transparent because of the distributed database technology. The Ethereum-based smart contracts would help to automate this process. Boardroom, an app, enables making decisions to take place on a blockchain. This means that company governance could become completely verifiable and transparent when handling information, digital assets, or equity.

File Storage

There are plenty of benefits when it comes to making file storage decentralized. When you share data across the network, it helps to protect the files from being lost or hacked. InterPlanetary File System (IPFS) makes it easy to see the way a distributed web could operate.

Some other uses of blockchain include:

- Intellectual property protection
- Internet of Things
- Identity management
- Data management
- Land title registration
- Stock trading

Chapter 3: Benefits and Challenges of Blockchain

One pioneer for using blockchain in cryptocurrency transactions has been the financial services industry. Blockchain is bitcoin's main technology. There have been 11 banks in the R3 consortium that have connected to Ethereum's blockchain network. Since 2013, the government of Estonia has used blockchain technology as a keyless signature infrastructure to verify data within their database.

Blockchain can increase data exchanges in different industries, too. It can make data transfer easier and simpler between people.

By using digital signatures on data that is run by blockchain, it gives access to authorized people that can regulate and maintain private health records. Insurance companies, patients, doctors, hospitals, and a whole community of people can be part of the blockchain to help reduce fraud within the healthcare system.

National security can be seriously compromised by unauthorized modification or access to the defense infrastructure like network firmware or operating systems. For many countries, computer systems and defense infrastructure are sent to multiple locations. By using blockchain technology throughout many data centers, it can help with security against attacks on equipment and networks by limiting access to modifications.

Departments of the government that work in storehouses can make exchanging information slower thus causing a negative impact on citizens. Synchronizing the data between departments by using blockchain will make sure the data gets released in real time, provided citizens and the departments agree to share the data. Blockchain technology can check corruption and improve transparency in governments all over the world.

Blockchains can hold huge amounts of data. This includes whole contracts. Smart contracts are going to have huge impacts on industries. Smart contracts are protocols that enforce contract performance by using blockchain. Smart contracts get rid of the middleman, like lawyers, since payments will occur due to certain aspects being met. Smart contracts can be easily enforced electronically. This creates powerful escrow by moving control from just one party. No one party needs to have complete control of a contract.

The newest trend in the power business is microgeneration of electricity. With microgeneration being added to traditional power supplies to create a new energy market. New initiatives like community solar power and generating home power are beginning to fill gaps in the power supply throughout the entire world. Smart meters can show how much electricity is consumed and produced within a blockchain. This lets the surplus energy get consumed in other locations and gives currency or credits to the original producer. These credits can then be transferred to the grid when the microgenerator needs to take electricity from the grid. The blockchain makes sure these contracts are in or near to real time. This lets the utility market be made with minimal red tape.

With all these possibilities, it isn't surprising that blockchain can improve the quality of how services are delivered, while enhancing the integrity and confidentiality of data. By promising to provide transparent and secure transactions, blockchain is poised to be a huge pillar of the world's digital technology.

Challenges

New services and products are being evolved by blockchain transactions. There aren't any regulations on how the transactions need to be written. Even though transparency and auditability are benefits of blockchain, industries that are extremely regulated might need to create new regulations for blockchain. Its ledger transactions will cause changes to industry regulations that govern auditing processes and financial reporting. For companies to protect their customers and investors, regulations will need to be changed. Laws are going to be put in place to govern smart contracts.

The service industry will play a critical role to make sure companies stick to government and industry regulations when they use blockchain.

Service providers have guaranteed assurance of continued updates to their customers.

We don't currently have one normal set of standards for writing blockchain transactions. There are three consortium organizations that have their own code and standards. This evolution is complicated by the various usages that blockchain has to offer. The standards will need to address these problems. The regulations that change to keep the environment regulated will help the adoption standards and could drive these consortiums together.

One more obstacle that executives fear about adopting this technology is that it hasn't been tested enough in POCs and pilots. What are the limitations of blockchain? Does it have the capability to handle huge volumes of data and transactions? Different applications will have different scalability problems as it gets adopted. How much computing power and time will it need to process numerous transactions?

Tamper-proof transactions can also be validated by blockchain's security. Some executives worry that private information on the blockchain can be shared. There are problems with this technology being trusted. Different vendors are trying to create strong security mechanisms and strong encryption. Consortiums and blockchain entities are trying out various methods to make sure that the technology can be trusted to protect private information.

The main challenge with adopting blockchain is that it is still a new technology. There are vulnerabilities and unknown factors. This is not going to stop blockchain from being adopted. Standards are going to be adopted, and regulations will be put in place. Critical changes will happen within the next few years that will show how blockchain can be applied to businesses. It will become easier to execute.

Just like any new technology that emerges, blockchain will have to evolve. Due to its disruptive power with all industries, it will potentially change very quickly. The service provider industry will be active in blockchain's adoption.

If you or your company is thinking about using blockchain to make your business more valuable, be sure you let the business drive this investment. You need to look at the needs or problems that your business might experience from blockchain and apply the technology accordingly. It won't work the other way around.

Chapter 4: The Basics of Bitcoin

Bitcoin came on the scene in 2008 after the "Occupy Wall Street" movement accused banks of charging extremely high fees, rigging the system, tricking clients, and misusing client's money. The pioneers of Bitcoin wanted to cut fees, hack corruption, make transactions transparent, get rid of the middleman, and put sellers in charge. They created a decentralized system. One that enables you to control your funds and constantly know what is happening with your money.

Problems can include delays with transactions, high volatility, and thieves hacking into accounts. People in underdeveloped countries might find that Bitcoin is a good option for receiving and giving money.

Bitcoin can be looked at as either digital currency, or it can reference the technology. Digital currency is a way to exchange digital information that lets you sell or buy services and goods. It gets its security by running a peer-to-peer network similar to a file-sharing system called BitTorrent or Skype.

Transactional Properties

- Permission: You don't have to ask to use cryptocurrency. It is software that anyone can download free of charge. Once it is installed, you can send and receive Bitcoins and other cryptocurrencies. Nobody can stop you.

- Secure: Bitcoins are locked inside a public cryptography system. The only person who can send cryptocurrency is the person who owns the private key. The magic of big numbers along with strong cryptography makes it impossible to break the code. A Bitcoin address has more security than Fort Knox.

- Global and Fast: Transactions are distributed almost instantly within the network and get confirmed in just minutes. Since this happens in a network of computers, there isn't any way of knowing your physical address. You can send Bitcoin to your next door neighbor or somebody in a completely different country.

- Pseudo-anonymous: Accounts or transactions can be connected to actual identities. You get Bitcoins on "addresses" that are chains of about 30 random characters. It is possible to analyze the transaction's flow; it isn't possible to find an actual identity of the person who is using this address.

- Irreversible: Once the transaction has been confirmed, it cannot be reversed by anybody. Your miner, Satoshi, president of your bank, not even you can reverse this transaction. If you send someone money, it has been sent. That's it. If you sent money to someone who has scammed you, it's gone. If someone was able to hack into your system and stole them from your computer, it's gone. You do not have a safety net.

How To Get Bitcoins

You can purchase your starting Bitcoins from these places:

- An exchange where you can use regular money for bitcoins. The common ones in Canada and the United States are LocalBitcoins, Gemini and Coinbase. In the United Kingdom, you can find them on Bittylicious and BitBargain UK.

- There are other cryptocurrency exchanges where you can change cash or Bitcoins for other cryptocurrencies like CoinCorner and BTER.

- Look on classified ads where you might find a seller who will trade your bitcoins for cash or even let you pay them in bitcoins. The most common site is LocalBitcoins.

47

- You can sell a service or product in exchange for bitcoins on sites like Purse.

NOTE: Bitcoin has been known for scams. Before you decide to use any service, look at reviews from other customer or ask questions on a Bitcoin forum.

How it Works

Bitcoin works on a public ledger called a blockchain. This is where all the transactions get confirmed and are included in blocks. As every block goes into the system, it is put into a peer to peer network of users to be validated. By doing this, all users know about every transaction. This prevents double spending and stealing. This process helps users to trust the system.

Unlike normal currencies that are issued by banks, Bitcoin doesn't have a central authority. It is a peer to peer network that is made up of machines like the networks that run Skype and BitTorrent. Bitcoins get generated mathematically as the network of computers executes difficult tasks. This is called mining. The mathematics in the system is set up so that it gets harder to mine with time. The total number of Bitcoins that will be mined is about 21 million. Central banks can't issue more Bitcoins to devalue the ones that are already in circulation.

How To Store Bitcoins

Before you begin to purchase Bitcoins, you need to set up a wallet to put your coins in. There are three different applications you can use:

- Web client: This looks like webmail since it relies on third-party servers. This third part server replaces an actual person and operates the whole transaction.

- Lightweight client: This would be an email client that is connected to a mail server to access a mailbox. It stores bitcoins but relies on a third party server to be able to access the network and complete the transaction.

- Full client: This is a standalone email server that handles everything about the process and doesn't have to rely on a third party. You have complete control on all your transactions from start to finish. This is not for newbies.

There are five types of wallets: Hardware, paper, web, mobile, and desktop.

How to Sell and Buy Things with Bitcoins

There isn't any way to trace Bitcoins the way you can actual dollars. You just have the transaction records that happen between addresses. Their balances will decrease and increase the records that get stored on blockchains.

Here is an example of a Bitcoin transaction:

Let's say you want to buy a collectible sword from someone. You are going to send them your private key. This is a sequence of letters and number that contain the person's digital wallet address, the amount you are sending them, and your source code. The receiver will scan a key with their smartphone to decode it. During this time, this transaction is broadcast to the entire network of participants on the ledger. About ten minutes later, the transaction is confirmed. This process will give the receiver a score to determine whether or not to accept this transaction.

Mining

Mining keeps the Bitcoin process secure by adding new blocks to the chain chronologically and keeping them in order. Blocks are added as every transaction gets finalized, Bitcoins get exchanged or passed, and codes get decoded.

Miners can make new bitcoins by using dedicated software to solve mathematical problems. This gives a secure way to issue currency and gives incentives for people who can mine.

The rewards are agreed-upon by all people within the network but are usually about 12.5 Bitcoins plus any fees paid by the user who sends the transactions. To keep inflation low and the system manageable, there can't be any more than a total number of 21 million Bitcoins circulating by 2040. This makes the puzzle harder to solve.

How To Protect Your Bitcoins

Just like you do with your everyday wallet, you must protect what's in it. You don't carry huge amounts of cash in it every day. You only carry small amounts of money to keep you safe. With your Bitcoins, you only want to keep small amounts of Bitcoins on your server, mobile, or computer for daily uses. Keep your remaining funds in a safe environment.

On a normal basis encrypt and backup your wallet by using a strong password. It won't protect you from keylogging software or hardware but will protect you from normal thieves.

Store your Bitcoins in a wallet that isn't connected to your network. This is called an offline wallet. You can think of this as being your bank since you try to keep some money in a wallet.

Keep your software updated. For additional protection, use multiple signature features that require multiple approvals before money can be spent.

Using these steps can protect your money.

Chapter 5: Ethereum

Ethereum software runs on a network of computers that makes sure smart contracts and data get processed and replicated on every computer within the network without needing a central facilitator. The vision behind it was to make a self-sustaining decentralized unstoppable computer.

It takes the blockchain concept from Bitcoin that replicates, stores, and validates data on several computers across the entire planet. This is where the term distributed ledger comes from. Ethereum takes this a step further and can run a code consecutively on several computers at one time on the whole planet.

Ethereum is about to do the same thing Bitcoin does for stored data, but Ethereum takes it one step further by adding in computations. The programs that are run are called smart contracts. These contracts are run by participants on their computer using a system called Ethereum Virtual Machine.

You can download Ethereum software called Ethereum client. You can write this yourself if you know coding and have the time and patience. Ethereum client connects by using the internet to connect to other computers that run the same software. You can begin to download the blockchain from the software so you can catch up. It validates each block independently to make sure it meets the Ethereum rules.

What can you do with the software? You can:

- Mine for new blocks
- Run smart contracts
- Create smart contracts and make new transactions
- Explore the blockchain
- Connect to the network

Your computer will become a node within the network. It will run an Ethereum Virtual Machine and work with the other nodes. Keep in mind that with a peer to peer network, there isn't a master server. All computers have equal status and power with the others.

Smart Contracts

These are programs that get stored on Ethereum's blockchain. They can be run by buying them with Ethereum.

You can set up a smart contract by setting up a new account and putting it on the blockchain with a transaction.

When the contract has been uploaded, and when you would like to run it, you make a transaction that contains a payment to the Ethereum contract. It might supply more information if the contract demands it.

Every mining computer runs the smart contract by using their Ethereum Virtual Machine as a part of the process. It will then reach a conclusion on the output. If everyone is aligned, every computer within the network will get the same conclusion since they are all running the same code with the information that has been supplied.

Each time a block is mined, the winning miner publishes the block to the entire network. The others will validate the same results, and add this to their blockchains. This is how the blockchain gets updated.

Orphans and Uncles

Ethereum can generate blocks faster than Bitcoin. Ethereum can mine 250 blocks each hour where Bitcoin can only mine six per hour. When blocks get created faster, the number of block clashes increases. Many valid blocks can be made at the same time, but just one will make it to the chain. The others lose, and their data isn't considered to be part of the ledger, even if the transactions are valid.

Bitcoin calls these blocks orphans. Ethereum calls them uncles. Uncles can be found by referencing subsequent blocks. Even though the data isn't used, there is a small reward for mining because they are still valid.

This helps to achieve two things:

1. It gives miners incentives to mine although there is a chance of making a non-mainchain block. The increased speed of creating blocks creates more uncles and orphans.
2. It increases the blockchain's security by noticing the energy that was spent making the uncle blocks.

ETH Units

One dollar can be broken down into 100 pennies. One bitcoin can be broken down into one hundred million satoshi. Ether, Ethereum's value token, can be broken down into Wei. There are one quintillion Wei in one Ether. It also goes by other names like Ada, Babbage, Shannon, Szabo, and Finney. These have been named after people who have made great contributions in the cryptocurrency field.

Ether and Wei are the most common denominations.

Timeline

Ethereum was a concept that Vitalik Buterin described in a White Paper in 2013. Dr. Gavin

Wood developed this concept and published his technical Yellow Paper in 2014. In July and August of 2014, a crowdsale fund occurred to fund development. Ethereum's blockchain was launched in July 2015. Ethereum has been developed and managed by many developers in the community.

The main vision of Ethereum was to build a censorship-resistant, decentralized, self-sustaining computer that can communicate, store data, and do calculations.

It has a permissionless, public open source and copies have been adapted to be used on private networks. The private and public versions try to solve different problems.

The technology is still immature but the more it is used, tested, developed, and built upon, the more it will continue to improve and become more robust.

Ethereum is the most exciting technology on the blockchain space.

Chapter 6: Consortiums

As financial institutions start exploring different possibilities of the blockchain technology, they are making systems that complement existing business models. A consortium or private platform allows them to stay private and maintain control while cutting down on costs and transaction speeds.

Private systems have faster speeds and lower costs that public platforms can't offer. Purists of the blockchain are not impressed. Private platforms kill their favorite part of the technology which is decentralization.

They see the private systems like big banks trying to gain control of the financial markets. They are correct for the most part.

If big banks can use blockchain technology to revolutionize finance, and they can pass the benefits on to customers, then it isn't evil.

Private Blockchain

The middleman comes back in with private blockchains, sort of.

It is better to stick with things you are familiar with than switching to something you aren't familiar with since the new things might be worse.

A company will write and verify every transaction. This allows greater efficiency and more transactions on the blockchain that can be completed faster. It doesn't offer decentralized security but trusting a business that runs on blockchain isn't any more dangerous than trusting one that doesn't.

The company gets to choose who has access to their blockchains, and this creates more privacy.

Competition is the main factor when developing useful products. Normal financial institutions have helped the monopoly within this industry. Their outdated services and products are the result of their power. Using a private version of this blockchain technology can push these organizations into the 21st century.

Most of our governing institutions are outdated and old, too. Our government, just like finance, isn't subject to competition. Integration and adoptions are slower, but if they could learn to adopt blockchain, it could cut out billions that are being spent behind the scenes.

Consortium Blockchain

A consortium blockchain is mostly private. There is some confusion about how it is different from a completely private system.

Instead of letting any one person who has an internet connection to verify transactions or letting one company have complete control, a few selected people or nodes are chosen.

This platform gives the same benefits as private blockchains like privacy and efficiency without using power from just one company.

Think of it as a council of elders. These members are known people, and they decide who has access to the ledgers.

The consortium platforms have most of the advantages of the private blockchain. They just operate being led by a group instead of just one person. This platform is great for collaborating with other organizations.

Think about central banks basing their activities on the international rules of finance. Or possibly the United Nations contracting out their voting system and transactional ledger to a blockchain system that allows every country to be a verifying node. There are endless possibilities.

Chapter 7: Industry Impact

You should now have a pretty good understanding as to what Blockchain is. It's easy to realize the ability the technology has to make the organizations that use it secure, efficient, decentralized, democratic, and transparent. It is probably going to end up disrupting a number of industries in the next five to ten years. Here are some of the industries that are already being disrupted.

Crowdfunding

Crowdfunding has now become a popular way to raise funds for new projects and startups in recent years. Platforms for crowdfunding exist to make trust between supporters and project creators, but they have a large fee. With blockchain-based crowdfunding, the trust is made through online reputation systems and smart contracts, which gets rid of the need for a middleman. New projects are then able to raise funds by releasing tokens that represent value, and that are able to be used later on for cash, products, or services.

Real Estate

Some of the biggest problems when it comes to selling and buying real estate are mistakes in public records, fraud, lack of transparency, and bureaucracy. When blockchain technology is used, it can speed up transactions by lowering the need to use paper-based record keeping. It can also be used for transferring property deeds, ensuring document accuracy, verifying ownership, and tracking. One such blockchain-secured real estate platform is Ubitquity.

Energy Management

The energy management industry has been highly centralized for a long time. Energy users and producers can't buy directly from each other, which forces them to use a trusted private intermediary or a public grid. There is an Ethereum-based startup, TransactiveGrid, that lets customers buy and sell energy directly from each other.

Healthcare

Healthcare is another industry that relies on legacy systems that are going to be disrupted by blockchain. A challenge that hospitals often face is the lack of a secure platform that they can share and store data on, and they tend to be the victim of hacking due to outdated infrastructure. With blockchain technology, hospitals are able to store data, such as medical records, safely and then share it with authorized patient or professionals. This will help data security and can help with the speed of diagnosis and accuracy. Tierion and Gem are two companies that are trying to upset the current data space for healthcare.

Government

The government systems tend to be opaque, slow, and prone to corruption. By using a blockchain-based system, it can reduce the bureaucracy and increases the transparency, security, and efficiency of government operations.

Voting

This is probably one of the most important parts of society that blockchain can disrupt. The 2016 US Presidential election was not the first time where parties have been accused of rigging the results. Blockchain technology could be used for electronic vote counting, identity verification, and voter registration. This will help to ensure that only the legitimate votes will be counted, and no votes are able to be removed or changed. Coming up with an immutable, publicly-viewable ledger of votes would be a huge step towards making the election system more democratic and fair. Follow My Vote and Democracy Earth are two startups that are looking to disrupt democracy itself by making a blockchain-based online voting system.

Ride Sharing and Private Transport

Blockchain can be used to make decentralized versions of peer-to-peer ridesharing apps. This would allow both car users and owners to arrange their own terms and conditions in a secure way without the need for third-party providers. La'Zooz and Arcade City are two startups working to make this happen.

Insurance

Trust management is the basis for the global insurance market. Blockchain provides a new way to manage trust. It can be used to verify lots of data types in insurance contracts, like the insured person's identity. Oracles can be used to integrate real-world data through smart contracts. This technology becomes extremely useful for insurance types that rely on real-world data.

Chapter 8: Free Blockchain Resources

It always helps to have some resources at your disposal when you are trying something new. Let's go over some interesting free resources across the blockchain ecosystem that will help you stay informed.

Factom University

Factom, Inc. came up with Factom University (https://www.factom.com/university/tracks) and is a growing knowledge base that was created to teach about blockchain, APIs, and the Factom platform. There you can find tutorials and videos that will turn you into an expert. They even have plans for a certificate program.

Ethereum 101

Ethereum community members started the website, Ethereum 101 (http://www.ethereum101.org/). It is a curated repository for information content about the Ethereum network and blockchain technology. Ethereum's Director of Community, Anthony D'Onofrio, oversees the website.

Build on Ripple

Ripple (https://ripple.com/build/) has come up with a robust knowledge base for building on their platform. This information is mainly geared for developers. They also have some resources that are made for financial regulators. It's a pretty good read even if you are not a regulator. It does give some insight into legal liabilities that could come with using blockchain technology.

Programmable Money

A Ripple employee, Steven Zeiler, has created a YouTube series (http://bit.ly/2DfLbVQ) on how you can make programmable money on Ripple's network with JavaScript. This is geared towards the JavaScript programmers.

Blockchain University

To learn more about the blockchain ecosystem, check out Blockchain University (http://blockchainu.co/). They provide information that helps teach entrepreneurs, developers, and managers about the ecosystem. They also offer private and public training programs, demo events, and hackathons. If you are looking for hands-on training, you can find them in Mountain View, California.

Bitcoin Core

Satoshi Nakamoto originally used Bitcoin Core (https://bitcoin.org/en/) to host their whitepaper on the Bitcoin protocol. It is now home to educational material on Bitcoin's core protocol, as well as downloadable versions of its original software.

Blockchain Alliance

The Blockchain Chamber of Digital Commerce founded the blockchain alliance (http://www.blockchainalliance.org/) and the organization Coincenter. It's a public-private collaboration with the regulators, blockchain community, and law enforcement.

Hivemind

Truthcoin was founded by Paul Sztorx, which is a peer-to-peer oracle system for Bitcoin. They use a proof-of-work sidechain that holds data on the state of prediction markets. Bitcoin is able to support smart contracts and financial derivatives through HiveMind (http://bitcoinhivemind.com/), which is a platform that was developed from Truthcoin's whitepaper. You can check out their educational materials and resources.

Chapter 9: Rules to Never Break on Blockchain

While blockchain is a useful and promising tool, there are some things that you shouldn't use it for. We are going to look at ten things that you should avoid doing while you are using blockchain and the cryptocurrencies that run them. It's helpful to have an attorney and CPA that you can consult before you make major financial decisions. This is still fairly new technology, and the rules that govern it have not been completely developed.

Blockchains or Cryptocurrencies should not be used to Skirt the Law

The legal zoning and legality of cryptocurrencies are still changing in different areas of the worlds.

- Are you able to use cryptocurrencies to hide money? This is a very dangerous idea. Keep in mind that blockchains keep records of every transaction forever, so if you believe that you have created a clever way to hide a few tokens, those that are trying to find bad behavior will be able to find it.

- Are you able to use blockchains as a way to smuggle money to different countries? There are a lot of countries that have limitations on the money that citizens can take from the country.

Blockchain keeps record of all of these transactions.

- Are you able to use cryptocurrency to buy illegal items? If you've noticed the pattern here, then you know that no, you can't. Blockchain keeps a record of all of your actions.

As a general rule, don't use your cryptocurrency or blockchain to do anything you wouldn't do with real money.

Contracts Need to Be Kept Simple

DAOs, decentralized autonomous organizations, chaincode, and smart contracts are popular at the moment. The chance to cut legal and administration cost is very enticing to a lot of corporations. An often overlooked characteristic of blockchain is the fact that it's only code. This means there are no humans interpreting the rules that you have written out for people to follow. The code becomes law, and this law will only stretch to what was worked into the blockchain contract. The 'fat' that you cut out can end up being very important.

You have nobody to interpret the code. This means if the code ends up being executed in a way that you didn't want, there is nobody to enforce the contract's intent. The code is the law and nothing unlawful has happened. That's the reason why you need to keep you contracts modular and simple in nature to predict and contain the outcomes of fulfillment. It also doesn't hurt to have your contract beaten up and tested by other developers who are promised something to break it.

Be Cautious When Publishing

The main point of a blockchain is once data is added; it's extremely hard to remove it. This means that anything you put in it will be around for a very long time. If you choose to publish encrypted sensitive data, you must be okay with the fact that your encrypted data could be broken and what you have published will then be readable to anyone.

People are working in cryptography to create a quantum proof encryption, but since quantum proof encryptions and quantum computing are still in their testing phase, it's hard to say what this technology will be able to do in 20 years time.

Make Sure Your Private Key Are Backed Up

Blockchains can be extremely unforgiving creatures. They don't care if you end up losing your passwords or private keys. There have been plenty of crypto nerds that have had to give countless tokens to the oceans of blockchain that will never get recovered.

Typically, your wallets are what control your cryptocurrency private keys. This is why it is so very important that you secure and protect them. You must be very careful with the online services that store your money for you. There are a lot of online wallets and cryptocurrency exchanges that have had their funds stolen.

You should only store a very small amount of tokens for everyday use in an internet-accessible device or online. You should view your cryptocurrency wallets like cash wallets. You should not keep more money in them than you are willing to part with at any given time. There are over a hundred known malware applications that are on the lookout to get your private keys and take your tokens.

The rest of your currency needs to be kept in cold storage, totally offline with no internet access. This may mean a paper wallet, a computer with no internet access, or a unique hardware device that was created to secure cryptocurrency.

Your digital wallets need to be backed up and stored in a safe place. The backup is in case your computer ends up failing, or you accidentally delete the wrong file. Your backup will let you recover your wallet if your device ends up being stolen or corrupted. You should also make sure that your wallet is encrypted. When you encrypt your wallet, it will let you set a password for withdrawing tokens.

When Sending Currency, Triple-Check the Address

A fair amount of scoundrels have been attracted to cryptocurrencies, so make sure you are careful when you send money. Once the money is out of your wallet, it is gone forever, and you can't get it back. You can't call up customer service, and there are no chargebacks. The money is gone.

Make sure you triple-check the wallet address before you send any money out. You want to know for certain that you send the money to the correct address.

Be Safe When Your Use an Exchange

Exchanges for cryptocurrency are the main points that hackers want to target to steal tokens. Hackers view them as a pot of gold ready for the picking, and over 150 of them have already been compromised.

You should keep this in mind when you use exchanges, and you need to follow the best practices to keep your tokens safe. You should research the exchange a little bit to figure out what their security measures are.

You should just use exchanges to move funds in and out. Exchanges should not be used to store value. You should hold significant amounts of cryptocurrencies in laminated paper wallets with several copies or cold storage.

Watch Out for Wi-Fi

If you didn't have your router set up correctly, there is a chance that somebody can see a log of your activity. If you use a public network, it's safe to assume that the network owner is able to see your activity.

You should only use trusted Wi-Fi networks. You should also make sure that you have changed the router password to a more secure password. For the most part, router passwords are set to factory default of 'admin' and anybody can easily overtake them.

Identify Your Blockchain Developer

The technology of blockchain is still new, and there aren't too many people that have a lot of experience when it comes to creating a blockchain application.

If you are interested in hiring a developer to help you with your project, check out their GitHub and look at the work they have done before you ever get started. They don't have to be experienced with blockchain specifically, but if they don't, then they need to be an extremely experienced developer outside of the world of blockchain.

Developers don't have too many resources at their disposal should they get stuck. Inexperienced developers will often struggle more and take longer to create the application.

Don't Get Tricked

As a whole, the blockchain industry doesn't have the same security and protection measures that banks and other financial institutions have. They also don't have the same laws to protect your financial welfare. They don't have consumer protection or FDIC bank insurance funds from the government. If you end up getting conned or robbed, you probably won't have anybody to turn to for help.

The industry also has a lot of hype in the last several years without all that much delivery of things of real value. 2016 saw more than a thousand new blockchain companies appear overnight that claimed expertise. When you are trying to develop a project, and trying to figure out if it's worth investment, it's best to take a second and make sure that it makes sense. You need to ask these questions:

- Are there any other tested technologies that you can use to accomplish the same thing with better efficiency?
- Is there value created in a way that benefits you?
- Is there real value created?

Blockchain technology has a lot of power and promise, which means it needs to be approached in a careful and thoughtful way.

Tokens Should Not Be Traded Unless You Know What You Are Doing

Cryptocurrencies tend to be volatile and swing wildly in their value at any given time, and oftentimes for no real reason. Most cryptocurrencies have very little depth, and trading a lot can end up crashing the market value. When you work with published blockchains, you will probably need to hold some of the currency to utilize them.

You should avoid getting caught up in trading tokens unless you have taken the time to understand their market. If you do end up making a choice to trade tokens, make sure you let your CPA know of your activity. You may have to report your losses or gains on your tax return.

Chapter 10: Top Blockchain Projects

Projects involving blockchain are frequently seen as a gamble, bearing in mind that we're talking about an industry that doesn't quite have a set future. Nevertheless, while blockchain may yet to be mainstream, it's important to note that more a billion dollars have been invested in it.

Investors and developers around the world quickly learned that blockchain can be useful to a lot of things more than just giving significant change to the financial system. That means that, as of this moment, the blockchain network has many amazing implications in several industries, including infrastructure, supply chain, government, energy, intellectual property, identity, financial, and more.

Let's look at the top five most ambitious and valuable projects that are based on blockchain that are currently available in the market, besides Bitcoin, which has been widely known in the market.

Ethereum

Since it was started, Ethereum has been in rollercoasters – going through ups and downs, but this project could be seen not only essential for smarter money but also to invincible smart applications. Knowing this, it depicts a platform that is decentralized and has sole purpose in running smart contracts. Smart contracts are applications that have high probability to run the exact way they were designed without having to deal with censorship, interference of third party, or downtime.

Many of the apps run on a custom-built blockchain, which are shared, huge, universal infrastructures that can't be messed with. This means that smart contract developers are able to transfer funds, make markets, and do several different tasks with no need of a mediator, or facing risks from any third-party.

Aside from this, crypto assets can be stored and created through the Ethereum wallet when you use Ethereum. The main objective of Ethereum currencies is to allow you to pay and deploy several smart contracts that the platform utilizes. This means whether you are interested in employing a trustless crowd sale for a project, coming up with a democratic organization with autonomy, creating your crypto-assets, or coming up with high-level decentralized applications, without a doubt, Ethereum can make it all easy for you.

Hyperledger

You may have heard what Hyperledger is especially if you have been keeping up with the recent blockchain and crypto news. It is not a project of its own, but Hyperledger is a great representation of a software effort that is open-source and is built from collaboration. It plans to allow developers to create advanced and multi-industry blockchain technology. This is more of a far-reaching collaboration that the Linux Foundation hosts, but is also hosted by many of the world's biggest leaders in things like the IoT (Internet of Things), banking, finance, manufacturing, technology, supply chain, and more.

You could view Hyperledger as a new high-level use for blockchain, which could fund a lot of the blockchain-based solutions and apps in the future. The success of the project is mainly based on the contributions and support of the developer community, as well as the supporting member companies. Getting started wouldn't be that hard especially if you have capital or idea.

Blockstream

Blockstream is very often referred to as a firm that is working on many different projects; among the top ones is helping speed up the projects that are based in cryptocurrency, as well as open-asset technologies and smart contracts. Since it came on the market, Blockstream is working not only to launch several side chain projects, but also Liquid, which is supposed to help make transfer times faster between the exchanges of Bitcoin.

In the past, Blockstream was able to manage grabbing around 55 million USD in Series A funding, which is a great help for the company to strengthen their protocol. This is while also working to help bring their projects up to a higher level.

Another great thing that Blockstream is working on is the Lightning Network – a project that would theoretically help make smaller Bitcoin transactions move faster through the blockchain. This may lead to faster confirmations as well as lower fees. Lightning Network would also help reduce the amount of transactions that are carried out off the blockchain.

Lisk

Often being compared to Ethereum, Lisk is actually quite different from it. One example is that it is written in JavaScript and is designed to run not on blockchains but Sidechains. This decentralized platform has worked to bring in more than 5,700,000 USD in funding. That means, they are getting prepared to launch an array of different services. The platform was built simple, therefore letting developers make their own apps a lot faster and with minimal effort. Currently, Lisk is collaborating with Microsoft to bring their platform to their Azure cloud, while they also integrating it on the Azure blockchain.

The main mission of Lisk is to help their users code, deploy, and use their personal applications, all while within the Lisk network.

Ripple

The main mission of Ripple is to change the current financial system of the world, while also starting what they call the 'Internet of Value.' Since global commerce is evolving rapidly and many businesses have become global, the expectations of users are also fast-growing. The payment infrastructure as of the present is not as good as it should be when it comes to newsfeed filling – which is where Ripple comes in. The company currently works with banks, and they are trying to use smarter technologies that are based on blockchain that is able to change the way that money is sent and received all over the world.

This means that the Ripple project is supposed to allow banks to send payments around the world and across networks in real-time. This is while also helping facilitate access to bank-based agreements; and lower cost, speed, and traceability of the funds.

It is extremely likely that we are going to hear more from these firms and projects in the near future. They continue to work on enhancing the way people network and can do their daily finance, while they also work on attaining a lot more efficient world.

Conclusion

Thank you for making it through to the end of *Blockchain: The Ultimate Guide to Understanding the Technology Behind Bitcoin and Cryptocurrency (Including Blockchain Wallet, Mining, Bitcoin, Ethereum, Litecoin, Ripple, Dash and Smart Contracts).* Let's hope it was informative and able to provide you with all the tools you need to achieve your goals.

The next step is to learn more about blockchain, and figure out how it can play a part in your life. Maybe you are looking to invest in cryptocurrencies, or you want to use smart contracts for your business. Blockchain has an increasing number of uses that will help to make your life easier.

Finally, if you found this book useful in any way, a review on Amazon is always appreciated!

Thank you!

Check Out Other Books

Please go here to check out other books that might interest you:

Bitcoin Investment Basics - Tips for Success
(Mastering Bitcoin for Starters)
by Leon Watson

How Do I Set Up My Kindle Fire HD: A Complete
Guide for Setting Up Your Kindle Fire HD Device
by Alex DaSilva

New Kindle Fire HD Manual (Kindle Fire HD 8
and 10)
by Corey Stone

Amazon Kindle Fire HD 10 Tablet Manual: The
Complete Kindle Fire HD 10 User Guide
(Troubleshooting, Tips and Tricks Included)
by Wesley Collins

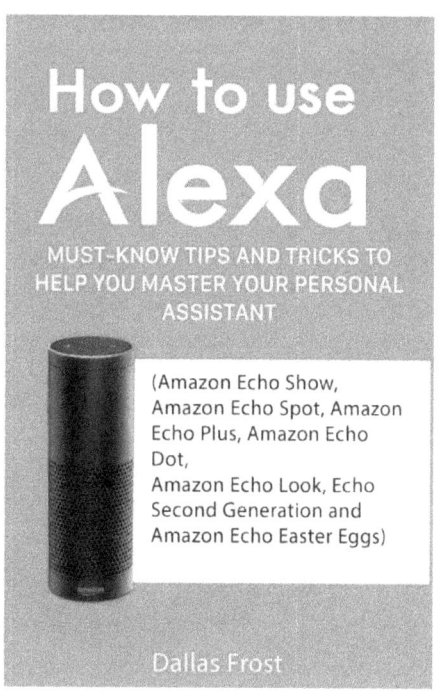

How to Use Alexa
by Dallas Frost

Best Seller

How to Delete Books from Kindle Devices
by Corey Stone

How to Add a Device to My Amazon Account
by Corey Stone

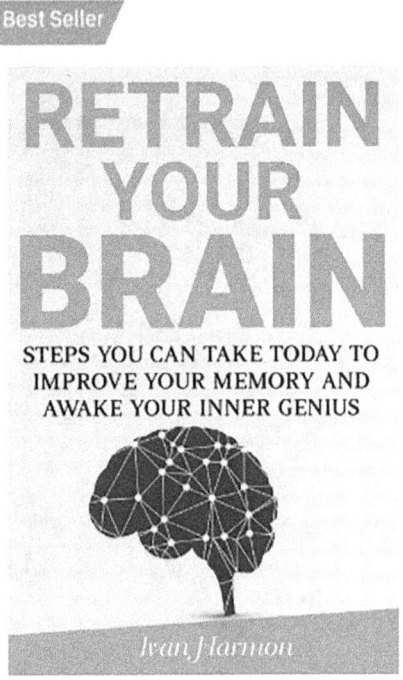

Retrain Your Brain: Steps You Can Take Today to Improve Your Memory and Awake Your Inner Genius by Ivan Harmon

Boost Your Brain Power: Learn Better, Smarter, and faster - Scientifically Proven Guides to Sharpen Your Focus and Retrain Your Brain by Ivan Harmon

What Your Boss Never Wants You to Know:
How to Find Your Strengths, Work Happier,
Grow Your Expertise, and Rediscover Your Life
by Lam Thanh Hue

www.ingramcontent.com/pod-product-compliance
Lightning Source LLC
Chambersburg PA
CBHW071251220526
45468CB00001B/77